The Trowel and the Truth

A Guide to Field Archaeology in the Holy Land

Second Edition

Scott Stripling

The Trowel and the Truth
A Guide to Field Archaeology in the Holy Land
Second Edition

Scott Stripling

Copyright © 2017 by Scott Stripling
ISBN: 978-1-61529-186-1

For information on reordering please contact:

Vision Publishing
P.O. Box 1680
Ramona, CA 92065
1-800-9-VISION
www.booksbyvision.org

Table of Contents

Illustrations

Tables

Figures

Foreword

Scott Stripling's *The Trowel and the Truth: A Guide to Field Archaeology in the Holy Land* gives readers a masterful treatment of the how and why of biblical archaeology. This book is important and timely for at least two reasons. First, archaeological work in the Holy Land continues to make good progress, resulting in exciting discoveries and fresh insights. Dr. Stripling's book informs readers of many of these recent and important discoveries. Secondly, archaeology greatly aids in the interpretation of Scripture. Few students, faculty, and pastors know the land of Israel and its rich treasures from the past as well as they should. Knowledge of the land and its archaeological insights will equip students, teachers, and pastors with important tools for better, sharper, more incisive interpretation of Scripture. Dr. Stripling's book shows how this can be done.

The Trowel and the Truth guides readers through every essential aspect of archaeology. This includes geography and chronology, which are vital for understanding the history of Israel, as well as the actual task of archaeological fieldwork and method. Knowing where and when major events took place provides the necessary context and makes it possible to interpret Scripture accurately. In a systematic way, Dr. Stripling's book then works its way through all the major periods in biblical history, from the pre-patriarchal and patriarchal eras to the Roman and Byzantine Ages.

Dr. Stripling articulates in the preface his understanding that "illumination of the Bible serves as the primary goal of ancient Near Eastern archaeology." He is of course quite correct. This is why the discipline is called "biblical archaeology." Some have objected to this language, arguing instead for something more neutral, but no one can deny that the desire to know the Bible better has historically been the driving force behind archaeology in the Near East. Without the correlation between the text of the Bible and the realia of the Near East, there simply would be no discipline called biblical archaeology.

Let me say that again: All the theological commitments in the world could never result in a field called "biblical archaeology" if no correlation between Bible and the remains of human culture could be found. And it has indeed been found, lots of it. It is because of great correlation between the biblical text and the results of archaeology that historians and biblical interpreters recognize that the Bible is talking about real people, real places, and real events. The Bible contains many parables and metaphors, to be sure, but the Bible contains lots of history, too. The work of Dr. Stripling and other archaeologists sheds light on this important history.

Dr. Stripling has studied under the guidance of the best. He has worked at several sites and in recent years has directed digs at significant places such as Khirbet el-Maqatir and Shiloh. Some of his finds are simply astounding. I remember the day I first visited Khirbet el-Maqatir. Dr. Stripling and his team had recovered the skeletal remains of eight persons who had died as the Roman army advanced on Jerusalem in the year AD 69. Desperate Jewish fathers and husbands tried to hide their wives and children in an underground olive press, but to no avail; the Romans found them and killed them. All that was left was ashes, debris, and bones. It was a graphic reminder of the cruelty of war.

To see the bones that were recovered from Khirbet el-Maqatir brought the past right into the present. To gaze upon the skeletal remains of these women and children, who lay unmourned and forgotten in an underground olive press for almost two millennia was sobering. In my opinion, this is one of the great values of archaeology: It brings the modern student and scholar face to face with the past. The past is no longer a story about a faraway place from a time long ago; the past becomes present, along with the joys and sorrows of those who lived in it, whose stories we want to hear afresh.

Dr. Stripling's clearly-written and well-illustrated book will help readers see the biblical past with new eyes and understand the biblical text with new insight. I welcome its appearance in a new and updated edition. *The Trowel and the Truth* deserves to be widely read. Those who read it will be enriched.

Craig A. Evans
John Bisagno distinguished professor of Christian origins
Houston Baptist University

Preface

In 2007, I released *The Trowel and the Truth* to serve not only as an introductory textbook on biblical archaeology for my students, but also as a guide to Bible readers who were interested in the relationship between artifact and text. Excavations over the last decade have yielded an enormous amount of new information on the material culture of the land of the Bible. This second edition updates the first, and it breaks much new ground as well, including new chapters on the pre-patriarchal eras and the postbiblical Byzantine Age. My own leadership role has expanded over the past decade. In 2014, I assumed the role of director of excavations at Khirbet el-Maqatir. And in 2017, on behalf of the Associates for Biblical Research, I opened a new excavation at the important site of Shiloh, under the auspices of the Civil Administration of Judea and Samaria. This second edition presents many of the findings at these significant sites in the highlands of Israel.

My presuppositions and biases will become obvious to the reader. I believe that God inspired the original biblical text, and that it has come down to the modern reader with an extremely high degree of accuracy. New manuscript fragments from the Dead Sea region continue to emerge, along with other ancient textual fragments, such as papier-mâché Egyptian death masks that contain possible remnants of the first-century Gospel of Mark.[1] I am pleased to see a growing number of textual scholars incorporating archaeological finds into their research and writings. Textual study and ancient Near Eastern archaeology must be seen as interdependent if we hope to enable the modern reader to appreciate the verisimilitude which was all too obvious to the ancient readers.

I am aware of the contemporary preference of many scholars to use BCE (before the Common Era) and CE (Common Era), but here I use the traditional BC (before Christ) and AD (*anno Domini*, in the year of our Lord) since the Common Era is a direct result of the birth of Christ, and my primary audience is the Christian community.

Throughout this book I strive to establish synchronisms (connections) between the biblical text and the physical remains of humans and their activities found in the archaeological record. These connections reinforce the discipline of Christian apologetics, that is, our defense of the faith. While archaeology plays a role in apologetics, the greatest benefit to the faith community exists in the illustrative nature of the discipline. In other words, *illumination of the Bible serves as the primary goal of ancient Near Eastern archaeology. By drawing out the cultural clues that are embedded in the remains of material culture, the text is set in its proper context.* Along the way, archaeology will likely "prove" many portions of the Bible, but we would do well to remember the words of Jesus: "If they do not listen to Moses and the Prophets, they will not be convinced even if someone rises from the dead" (Luke 16:31).

The value of archaeology in biblical studies remains a lifelong passion for me, so the writing of this book has been a labor of love. I hope that the reader will sense my passion and return to his or her Bible reading with a renewed sense of awe and devotion and with new tools and lenses.

The footnotes provide further insights or explanations, and at times, suggestions of where to look to learn more about a topic in question. The bibliography includes works from which I have benefitted or that I consulted during my writing. While I do not agree with everything written by every author, these books represent mainstream scholarship on the archaeology and history of the ancient Near East. At the end of each chapter, I set forth some questions for further study and discussion. It would serve the reader well to peruse these questions before reading the chapter in order to anticipate important concepts. My pedagogical training has taught me that most people are visual learners, so I have included more pictures than are typically found in a book this size.

An archaeologist should vigorously engage the scholarly community, something in which I am actively involved through peer-reviewed journals, conference presentations, and forthcoming volumes of the final publication of my excavations. But, *this book is not written for scholars*. I have targeted two audiences. The first is the faith community to which I have the privilege of addressing in various churches and conferences throughout the year. They have expressed an enormous enthusiasm for the light that the spade sheds on the Scriptures, or perhaps more appropriately, the light that the trowel sheds on the truth. The second is my students and archaeological volunteers whose passion to understand Scripture and change the world never ceases to amaze and motivate me.

Acknowledgements

I am indebted to many people who have helped me with this project and in my career. Dr. Steven Collins gave me my first archaeological supervisory opportunity at Tell el-Ḥammam where I worked for six seasons and learned a tremendous amount. My colleagues at the Associates for Biblical Research have been instrumental in any success that I have had. I learned much from Dr. Bryant Wood who preceded me as the director of the Khirbet el-Maqatir excavations. We all owe a debt of gratitude to Dr. Wood for his research on Jericho and Ai. Scott Lanser, Henry Smith, and Gary Byers provided unwavering encouragement and support. My entire excavation staff continually expends themselves beyond my expectations, and they deserve recognition for their tireless work.

Dr. Craig Evans graciously wrote the foreword to this second edition. He is the John Bisagno distinguished professor of Christian origins at Houston Baptist University and a prolific author on the person of Jesus and the background of the New Testament. Michael Luddeni, Steven Rudd, and Dr. David Graves of Liberty University generously provided photos, and Dr. Leen Ritmeyer created many of the amazing graphics. Michael Sanchez produced the brilliant cover designs for both the first and second editions. Dr. Mark Hassler from Virginia Beach Theological Seminary edited the manuscript. Any errors that remain are mine, not his. I am privileged to know these men as colleagues and personal friends.

Finally, my dear wife Janet has tirelessly supported my efforts, never once complaining about the holidays, anniversaries, and birthdays that I have missed in my pursuit of digging the Bible. To her, I am most grateful.

Archaeology is not a science; it is a vendetta.

❖ Mortimer Wheeler

Chapter 1

Geography and Chronology

Over one billion Christians worldwide base their lives and daily decisions on the Bible. In addition, over one billion Muslims and millions of Jews find faith connections in the places mentioned in the Bible. Only a small percentage of these believers will ever have the opportunity to visit the Holy Land, where many of the stories occurred which they venerate and base their faith upon. As a result, their own cultural and geographical limitations often cloud their understanding of the events of the Bible. For example, a person from Texas tends to visualize the cities mentioned in the patriarchal narratives of Genesis as being far apart. After all, a person in Houston cannot see Dallas, nor can a person in San Antonio see Austin. By contrast, the land of the Bible is diminutive, more like the size and shape of New Jersey. From Bethel or Shechem, where the patriarchs spent considerable time, other biblical cities could be easily viewed.[2] Before we delve into the archaeology of the Bible, it will be helpful to get a handle on the geography and topography of the Levant since these factors directly influenced the development of a number of civilizations, including the Canaanites, Amorites, Israelites, Philistines, Ammonites, Moabites, and Edomites.

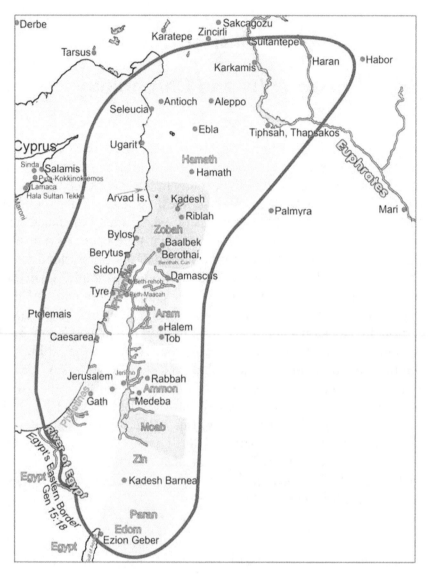

Figure 1.1. Traditional boundaries of Israel's united kingdom

The boundaries of the Levant vary from one scholar to the next, but this area generally refers to the land on both sides of the Jordan River, extending to the Nile Delta in the south and the Euphrates

River in north. The term *Palestine* more narrowly describes the area of modern Israel and Jordan. Herodotus used the term in the fifth century BC. In response to the Second Jewish Revolt of AD 132–135, Hadrian adopted Herodotus' terminology and named Judea *Palestina*, meaning, the land of the Philistines. This pejorative term elevated Israel's ancient nemesis and essentially denied the relevance and land rights of Abraham's descendants. According to archaeologist Amihai Mazar,

> Palestine, in fact, should be considered part of the more extensive region generally denoted "the Levant," including Palestine, Lebanon, and the western half of Syria (the Orontes Valley and the region of Aleppo), which have various common geographic and climatic features. The Levant's southern part, comprising Palestine, Lebanon, and southern Syria, constitutes a homogeneous unit which conforms to the biblical definition of the Land of Canaan.[3]

In general terms, the land of the Bible encompasses the Fertile Crescent, from the Persian Gulf in the southeast to the Khabur Triangle in the north, to Egypt in the southwest. The missionary activities of the apostles and others in the New Testament greatly expanded the geographic context of the biblical narratives, taking in Asia Minor and Europe.

Mesopotamia and Egypt were places of captivity and slavery for the Hebrew people. Practically speaking, when people refer to the Holy Land, they refer to the narrow strip of land east of the Mediterranean Sea. The land between the Euphrates River and the River of Egypt was promised to Abram's offspring in Genesis 15:18. Under David and Solomon, Israel appears to have briefly possessed the land in its entirety, except for a few pockets of resistance (fig. 1.1).

The land of the Bible divides into several different geographical zones. Each zone had a unique microclimate, and at times, its own subculture or subcultures.

The Jordan River

The Jordan River served an important role in ancient times. It functioned as the main water artery for the region. The headwaters of the Jordan begin on Mount Hermon, near the current border of Israel and Lebanon. The Old Testament evokes Mount Hermon, and specifically, "the dew of Hermon" (Ps 133:3). The dew refers to the moisture and melted snow that seeps through the porous rocks and becomes the northernmost stretch of the river. The river meanders for about twenty miles before entering Lake Hula, a small body of water. Josephus, the first-century Jewish historian, referred to it as Lake Semichonitis. Today, a marsh replaces the ancient lake. Nearby sits Abel Beth-Maacah, the stronghold that Joab besieged in quest of Sheba.

The river continues south for another twenty miles before emptying into the Sea of Galilee, also known as Lake Tiberias. The sea measures roughly 7.5 miles wide and 13 miles long. From the outlet, near the ancient site of Khirbet Kerak, the water flows sixty-five miles as the crow flies until it finally enters the Dead Sea. Josephus refers to the Dead Sea as Lake Asphaltis because of its bitumen, a naturally occurring substance.

By the time the water reaches the Dead Sea, it is little more than a creek because of irrigation systems and modern dams.[4] In biblical times, the width of the Jordan would vary from one hundred feet or so to more than a mile at flood stage. The water surged at flood stage when the Israelites crossed to begin the conquest of Canaan. The people crossed opposite Jericho. The river had stopped flowing about fifteen miles upstream of Jericho, in the vicinity of Adam (Josh 3:16). The crossing occurred near Bethabara (the place of crossing) or Bethany (the place of the ship). The Gospel of John refers to the site as "Bethany beyond Jordan." There John baptized his cousin Jesus (John 1:26–28). This is a prescient point—Jesus was baptized at the place where the Israelites crossed into the promised land. Also near this spot, a flaming chariot transported the prophet Elijah (2 Kgs 2:11) (fig. 1.2).

At times, the Jordan River acted as a barrier that separated different cultures; at other times, it served as a bridge that

Figure 1.2. Jordan River

connected them. After the Early Bronze Age (3200–2350 BC), rainfall in the Levant drastically decreased.[5] As a result, the Jordan became the most important and reliable source of fresh water for the inhabitants of the rift valley during the biblical periods. Other sources of water included springs, wadis, wells, and aqueducts. Rainfall could be collected in cisterns, large pithoi, or the like.

The Jordan Rift Valley

Prior to the patriarchal period, a huge rift valley formed from north of Lebanon to Mozambique in central Africa. The rift separates the African and Arabian tectonic plates. An upheaval in the surface of the earth left this huge scar, thus creating the low places that form the basins for Lake Hula, the Sea of Galilee, and the Dead Sea. Water likely filled the entire rift from the Gulf of Aqaba to Mount Hermon. Over time, the waters receded and evaporated, leaving only the three bodies of water just mentioned.

The largest of these seas, the Dead Sea—and the surrounding Dead Sea basin—drops thirteen hundred feet below sea level, the lowest elevation on earth. The low elevation creates the illusion that the surrounding mountains rise higher than they actually do. The Transjordanian mountains, east of the Jordan River, rise thirty-five hundred feet above sea level, about one thousand feet higher than their Cisjordanian counterparts west of the Jordan. From thirteen hundred feet below sea level, the mountains appear to be a mile high.

Throughout history, the Dead Sea has remained about seven miles wide and about twenty-four miles long. But recently, due to low water levels, the northern and southern sections of the sea have been partially separated by the Lisan Peninsula. Much of the southern end dried up, except for occasional pools.[6]

William F. Albright, often referred to as the father of ancient Near Eastern archaeology, along with others, suggested in the 1930s that the lost cities of Sodom, Gomorrah, and the other cities of the plain sat under the waters at the southern end of the Dead Sea. As I will discuss later, his theory proved incorrect, although many ancient people groups did settle along the southern shore. The Early Bronze Age sites of Bab edh-Dhra῾ and Numeira exemplify such settlements.

About three miles northeast of the Dead Sea, Chalcolithic settlers established the large site of Teleilat el-Ghassul. Jesuit archaeologists Alexis Mallon and Robert Koppel first excavated this site prior to the Second World War. Other large Chalcolithic settlements centered in the Golan region, near the Yarmuk River, and on the west side of the Dead Sea at ῾Ein-Gedi. Ample rainfall made these large and ancient settlements sustainable until the end of the Early Bronze Age (ca. 2350 BC). A reduction in precipitation contributed to the smaller cities in the Middle Bronze Age (1950–1483 BC) and the even smaller cities of the Late Bronze Age (1483–1177 BC).

West of the Jordan River

About two-thirds of the events of biblical history occurred west of the Jordan River. The Cisjordan area lies between the Mediterranean Sea on the west and the Jordan River on the east. The northern border varied from time to time. Sometimes it was near Mount Hermon, but in the time of David and Solomon it reached to the Euphrates River. The River of Egypt might have served as the southernmost boundary, but more commonly, the boundary reached only to the Negev, near Beersheba and Arad.

The Central Hill Country

Figure 1.3. Agricultural terracing

The earliest Israelite settlements emerged in the highlands or central hill country, the high ridge or spine that extends from Shechem in the north to Hebron in the south. Shiloh became the most important site in this newly-settled area due to its role as the centralized religious center. Hundreds of new Israelite settlements appeared in the highlands in the late thirteen century BC. The transition from a nomadic to a sedentary lifestyle lasted two centuries. During this time, some Israelites continued to live in tents, while others moved into the Canaanite and Amorite homes in the cities which they conquered (cf. Deut 6:10–11). The heavily forested areas required extensive clearing in order to be farmed. The sedentary life also necessitated a new technology called terracing. Terracing transformed a hillside into flat and farmable land by creating stair-step type ledges, six to thirty feet wide (fig. 1.3). Terracing prevented the valuable topsoil from washing into the valleys. Residents of the hill country were geographically isolated from the other population centers and tended to be culturally isolated as well.

Since there were no rivers or lakes on the high ridge of the hill country, cities were built near natural springs, or the inhabitants would dig wells or cisterns in order to create a reliable water supply (fig. 1.4). Most Israelites had access to a spring within a mile of their village. The most notable water source in this region was the Gihon Spring in Jebus (Jerusalem). David exploited this water source in order to enter the Jebusite city. And Hezekiah advanced a massive municipal project to redirect the water inside the city walls. The famous Siloam Inscription corresponds with the biblical and apocryphal accounts (2 Kgs 20:20; 2 Chr 32:30; Sir 48:17–18).[7]

Figure 1.4. Plastered cistern at Khirbet Qumran

In addition to water availability, the size of a settlement was affected by defensibility and access to transportation and trade routes. Elevations ranged from two thousand to almost four thousand feet, and precipitation levels ranged from abundant to sparse as one moved from north to south.

The Coastal Plain

The coastal plain stands in stark contrast to the hill country. This coveted region boasts rich alluvial soil and even seaports, which were essential for trade. Natural coves or inlets at Acre, Jaffa, and Dor functioned as seaports. The coastline did not have a true harbor until the late first century BC, when Herod the Great built a magnificent harbor at Caesarea by sinking barges filled with concrete. Herod dedicated the harbor to his patron, Caesar Augustus. Herod's harbor became the most impressive harbor in the entire Roman world.[8]

Some cities, such as Ashkelon, have been around since the Early Bronze Age. Aphek also played a prominent role in the region. The well-known sharon plain lies north of the Yarkon River and the modern city of Tel Aviv (cf. Song 2:1).

North of the sharon region, the coastal plain narrows considerably near Mount Carmel, before widening again by the mountains of Lebanon. Around 1177 BC, the Philistines and other Sea Peoples gained control of the coastal plain and became arch-adversaries of the Israelites. Both groups attempted to exert hegemony over the region.

A famous highway, the *Via Maris* (the road by the sea), ran through the coastal plain and connected Egypt with Mesopotamia. Battles often occurred near the coastal cities because rulers desired to control the highway and trade routes. Megiddo, where many battles were fought in antiquity, stands out as a prime example. One of the more famous battles happened there in 1482 BC when the powerful Thutmose III defeated an alliance of regional kings. Inscriptions in the temple of Amun at Karnak document the details.

The Shephelah

Between the central hill country and the coastal plain lay another distinct geographical region known as the Shephelah. The Shephelah, comprised of rolling hills, descends gradually from the highlands to the coast. The rich alluvial soil mixes with the sandy soil from the coast (loess or rendzina soil). A mixture of soils contributes to the abundant harvests. The Shephelah is subdivided by a number of east-west valleys, such as the Aijlon Valley, where Joshua performed his military exploits, and the Elah Valley, where David defeated Goliath. The more important cities in the foothills included Gezer, Azekah, Lachish, Beth-Shemesh, Maresha (Beit Guvrin), and Timnah (Tel Batash, cf. fig. 1.5).[9] Near Beit Guvrin is Tel Burna (biblical Libnah?), currently under excavation.[10]

East of the Jordan River

Figure 1.5. Seal impression from Timnah (*lmlk*, belonging to the king)

Approximately one-third of the Holy Land lies east of the Jordan River. This area, known as the Transjordan, is divided by three rivers or gorges: the Yarmuk, the Jabbok, the Arnon, and the Zered (from north to south). As mentioned, large Chalcolithic communities flourished near the Yarmuk River, and further south at Teleilat el-Ghassul, three miles or so northeast of the Dead Sea.

Both the Early and Middle Bronze Ages are represented at Pella and Tell el-Ḥammam. Pella was also occupied in the Late Bronze Age. Recent excavations at Tell el-Ḥammam by Steven Collins of Trinity Southwest University have fueled speculations that the site was the biblical city of Sodom.[11] However, the massive destruction layer dates to about 1650 BC and does not fit any mainstream chronology for the destruction of Sodom. I worked as a square supervisor and field supervisor in the first six seasons of excavation (fig. 1.6). While the Sodom identification remains problematic, I agree with a number of scholars who identify Tell el-Ḥammam as the site of Shittim, the place where the Israelites last encamped before beginning the conquest of Canaan (Num 25:1; Josh 2:1; 3:1). David Graves and I make a strong case that the early Roman and Byzantine remnants at the site represent the first-century city of Livias.[12]

Figure 1.6. Scott Stripling (*bottom center*) and others at Tell el-Ḥammam

Prior to the arrival of the Israelites, many nations lived east of the Jordan: the Bashanites, the Ammonites, the Moabites, the Edomites, and the Midianites (from north to south). Two and a half of the Israelite tribes did not permanently cross over to Canaan—namely, Reuben, Gad, and half of Manasseh (fig. 1.7). Sparse settlements populated the eastern side of the Jordan, thus making it easier for the Israelite tribes to settle the region. The Mesha Stele, also called the Moabite Stone, was discovered in 1868 near Dhiban. It dates to the ninth century BC, and it documents the existence of the tribe of Gad in the region of Moab. It fits precisely with Numbers 32:34–36, and is an example of a synchronism—a convergence of the biblical text and the archaeological data.

Iron Age materials exist at many sites in Transjordan, including Tell Deir ʿAlla, Tell el-Ḥammam, Tell Kefrein, Tell el-ʿUmayri, Khirbet el-Medeineh, Khirbet en-Nahas, and Tell Jalul. Andrews

University currently excavates at Tell Jalul under the leadership of Randy Younker, Connie Gane, Paul Ray, and Paul Gregor.

Figure 1.7. Settlement of the Israelite tribes in Canaan

The Babylonians, Persians, and Greeks largely ignored the east side, but the Romans built impressive structures around the region

Figure 1.8. Aqueduct at Tell el-Ḥammam, Jordan

beginning in the first century BC. The structures include bathhouses, amphitheaters (e.g., at Amman), and temples (e.g., at Jerash), and aqueducts (fig. 1.8).

Some important archaeological studies east of the Jordan deserve mention. The first person in the modern era to do extensive survey work east of the Jordan was a student and colleague of W. F. Albright, Nelson Glueck. Glueck spent considerable time there in the 1930s. His prescient and addictive writings on Jordan give rise to the expression, "gripped by Glueck." Moreover, in 1975 and 1976, the Jordanian Department of Antiquities sponsored an important regional survey. Perhaps the most comprehensive book on the archaeology of this region remains Rami Khouri's *The Antiquities of the Jordan Rift Valley*.

In antiquity, the King's Highway functioned as the most important transportation artery east of the Jordan River (cf. Num 20:17; 21:22). Like the *Via Maris* in the coastal plain, ancient peoples went to great lengths to control the King's Highway in order to benefit from trade opportunities. For example, the Nabateans, who flourished from about 200 BC to AD 200, built the amazing city of Petra and exercised monopolistic control over the frankincense trade (fig. 1.9).[13] The wise men of Matthew 2:14 traveled from the east, possibly to Petra. From there, they would have traveled along the King's Highway before crossing over to Bethlehem. After the exodus, the Israelites spent some time at

Petra, then called Rekem. This southern portion of the Levant, along with the entire Sinai Peninsula, was a rugged desert with a sparse population.

Figure 1.9. Temple of Treasures at Petra

Archaeological Time Periods

For the sake of analysis and discussion, archaeologists categorize the physical remains of ancient cultures into different time periods. Danish archaeologist Christian Thomsen (1788–1865) introduced the three-age system. He related the classification of artifacts to technology—technology involving stone, bronze, and iron. The Stone Age refers to the period in which tools and weapons were primarily made of stone, prior to the widespread use of metals.[14] The Bronze Ages are the periods in which people mastered bronze. The Iron Age corresponds roughly to the invention and introduction of iron technology. Of course, there are exceptions. Iron implements, for example, have been found in the Late Bronze

Age. Obviously, the anthropological changes occurred gradually and in a fluid manner. Archaeologists also identify archaeological time periods by ethnic descriptors such as the Canaanite period (the Bronze Age) and the Israelite period (the Iron Age). Table 1.1 displays the generally accepted dates for ancient Near Eastern archaeology as it relates to the Bible.

Table 1.1. Archaeological dates for Palestine, as commonly accepted

10,000–4500	Neolithic Age
4500–3200	Chalcolithic Age
3200–2350	Early Bronze Age
2350–1950	Intermediate Bronze Age (EB IV–MB I)
1950–1483	Middle Bronze Age
1483–1177	Late Bronze Age
1177–587	Iron Age
587–332	Babylonian and Persian Ages (Iron Age IIC or Iron Age III)
332–63	Hellenistic Age
63–325	Early Roman Age
325–636	Late Roman and Byzantine Ages
636–1099	Early Islamic Age
1099–1291	Crusader Age

In addition to the archaeological periods in the table, further subdivisions have resulted from closer analysis. For example, the Iron Age divides into Iron Age I (1177–950 BC) and Iron Age II (950–587 BC). These time periods break down even further. Iron Age IIC, for instance, refers to the period of the Babylonian conquest and ultimately the destruction of Jerusalem and the surrounding cities in 587 BC.

According to LXX chronology, a flood occurred in the lifetime of Noah, around 3200 BC. This dating of the flood assumes that Abraham was born in 2166 BC, and that the Genesis record uses a gap-less genealogy from Noah to Abraham. If the flood covered the entire planet, there could be evidence of it in the archaeological strata of the Levant. To my knowledge, no such evidence exists in the Levant, although a re-examination of the appropriate strata at key sites would be an important undertaking. My colleague, Henry

Smith, posits that the cataclysmic proportions of the flood completely dismantled the antediluvian cities.

To buttress Smith's theory, I suggest a tentative chronology. The earliest archaeological stratum, the Neolithic stratum, began around 3200 BC. Abraham dates within one hundred years of 2000 BC. Can the Early Bronze, Chalcolithic, and Neolithic periods be compressed into twelve hundred years? To test this hypothesis, numerous sites will need to be re-examined. However, three archaeological periods can fit nicely into a 1,200-year span. For example, the Intermediate, Middle, and Late Bronze Ages together equal 1,173 years. In fact, any combination of three periods after the time of Abraham fit easily within a 1,200-year span. Table 1.2 shows my tentative chronology.

Table 1.2. Archaeological dates for Palestine, according to Stripling

3200–2850	Neolithic Age
2850–2500	Chalcolithic Age
2500–2150	Early Bronze Age
2150–1900	Intermediate Bronze Age (EB IV–MB I)
1900–1483	Middle Bronze Age
1483–1177	Late Bronze Age
1177–587	Iron Age
587–332	Babylonian and Persian Ages (Iron Age IIC or Iron Age III)
332–63	Hellenistic Age
63–325	Early Roman Age
325–636	Late Roman and Byzantine Ages
636–1099	Early Islamic Age
1099–1291	Crusader Age

Note: Early dates based on Smith's hypothesis.

If Smith's hypothesis doesn't hold water, Noah's flood may have only covered the Black Sea region. There are five places in the Bible where "the whole world" does not appear to mean the entire planet (1 Kgs 10:24; Zeph 3:8; John 12:19; Col 1:6; Rom 1:8). Thus, a plausible argument can be made from Scripture for a major regional flood in the ancient world. This would potentially explain the lack of flood evidence in the archaeological record of the Levant.

Further Study and Discussion

What were the water sources in the Levant during Bible times?

What were the benefits of terracing, and what motivated its development?

What two major roads facilitated travel in the Levant in antiquity? How did these roads influence the settlement and movements of people?

What arguments support a universal flood? What arguments support a regional flood?

There are rest and healing in the contemplation of antiquities.

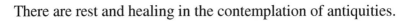 Mark Twain

Chapter 2

Archaeological Fieldwork and Methodology

The popular images of Indiana Jones and Lara Croft could not be further from reality when it comes to what archaeologists actually do. These larger than life Hollywood characters operate alone, whereas archaeologists work in teams. While there have been treasure hunters and tomb robbers like Jones and Croft since the beginning of time, archaeology as a discipline only began 150 years ago. The following excerpt appeared in a 2006 issue of *Biblical Archaeology Review*:

> In Samuel Johnson's monumental dictionary, composed between 1746 and 1755, he defined archaeology (spelled "archaiology") merely as "a discourse on antiquity." Henry Hitchings, in *Defining the World*, tells us that "in Johnson's mind, and in the estimate of most of his peers, it [archaeology] was associated with the quaint antiquarianism of dilettanti, and was an amateur pursuit, not science."[15]

Only within the last 120 years have biblical commentaries begun to reflect the fruitful dialogue between biblical studies and archaeology. An exception to this recent interest occurred in the sixth century BC. Nabonidus, the final Babylonian king of antiquity, partially excavated (or dug up) several ancient cities such as Ur, according to the Sippar Cylinder (fig. 2.1). But Nabonidus' fascination with the past does not match the modern understanding of archaeology.

Figure 2.1. Sippar Cylinder of Nabonidus

Major Personalities in Archaeology

A number of travelers traversed the land of the Bible during the Byzantine period (AD 325–636) and Arab period (after AD 636). The travelers were normally interested in visiting sites such as Bethlehem, Nazareth, and Jerusalem because of the connection to the Bible. The pilgrim of Bordeaux and the Spanish pilgrim Egeria furnish important early accounts. Egeria maintained a detailed diary of her explorations on both sides of the Jordan.[16] In 1611, William Lithgow of Scotland visited the region and kept a diary of his travels.[17] In 1842, Ida Laura Pfeiffer traveled through the Levant and Egypt and published her journals under the title, *A Visit to the Holy Land, Egypt and Italy*.[18] These and other pilgrimages, such as Mark Twain's visit in the late nineteenth century, resulted in a great deal of western curiosity.

A watershed event occurred in 1799 when Napoleon Bonaparte conquered Egypt and most of the Near East, thus allowing western investigation of biblical sites for the first time since the Crusades of the late eleventh to late thirteenth centuries.

Napoleon came to Egypt with a team of scientists, artists, cartographers, and others. One of his engineers found the Rosetta Stone, a trilingual inscription that unlocked ancient Egyptian hieroglyphics (fig. 2.2). This and other discoveries fueled the already intense desire of European nations such as Germany, England, Holland, and France to visit and identify biblical sites. Later, the Americans would come to play a dominant role in archaeology,

Figure 2.2. Rosetta Stone

and ultimately the Israelis, Palestinians, and Jordanians would produce their own leaders and scholars in the field.

Edward Robinson

One of the first Americans to travel to the Levant was Edward Robinson, a biblical scholar and geographer. He arrived in 1836. Robinson did very little actual excavation, but his keen observations resulted in vastly superior Bible maps that advanced the work of future archaeologists. Today, the remains of an archway at the southwest corner of the Temple Mount in Jerusalem bear the name "Robinson's Arch" because he first observed its upper portion protruding through the ground (fig. 2.3). What Robinson thought to be the bottom of the archway actually turned out to be the top. No one had imagined that thirty-six feet of dirt could have accumulated in only eighteen hundred years. Nineteenth–century lithographs reveal the extent to which the

Figure 2.3. *Left,* Robinson's Arch reconstructed; *right,* Robinson's Arch today

retaining walls of Herod's Temple Mount platform were covered with accumulated debris. The same area is now completely excavated.

Robinson and his contemporaries—Claude Conder, Herbert Kitchener, Charles Wilson, Conrad Schick, Charles Claremont-Ganneau, and others—did not differentiate the many hills in the Levant from actual archaeological tells, stratified hills that grow from centuries of occupation. That is where Flinders Petrie comes in.

Flinders Petrie

America's third president, Thomas Jefferson, observed basic stratification while probing Native American mounds at his Monticello estate in Virginia. But it was Flinders Petrie who initially developed stratigraphic study in the Holy Land (fig. 2.4). In 1890, Petrie identified stratigraphy at Tell el-Ḥesi in the southeastern portion of the Levantine coast. A decade earlier, Petrie had become famous for his scientific measurements of the Egyptian pyramids. He gained access to the pyramids by extremely creative and unconventional means. He dressed up as a woman and pretended to be crazy, living in a tomb while doing his archaeological work. At Tell el-Ḥesi, Petrie observed the change in the material culture as he excavated deeper into the tell. He compared the ceramic assemblages in order to date the various strata. This led to a more careful approach among future archaeologists.

Petrie developed a method of sequence dating that used a numbering system of one to one hundred. Numbers were assigned to the different ceramic types in order of appearance, starting from the bottom of the tell. This provided an absolute chronology for the ceramic

Figure 2.4. Oil portrait of Flinders Petrie

types. Eventually, ceramicists could compare the ceramic types with Egyptian artifacts of known dates, and thereby deduce approximate calendar dates for the ceramic types.

Three decades after his important work at Tell el-Ḥesi, Petrie returned to the same region to probe several smaller tells in what would become the first attempt at a regional (rather than local) approach to archaeology. Modern archaeologists, following Petrie, normally excavate with a regional awareness and sensitivity. Both the Associates for Biblical Research and the Madaba Plains Project excavate multiple sites in their respective regions in order to obtain a broader perspective of the material remains. Even in death, at age eighty-nine, Petrie remained eccentric. He left instructions to bury his body in the Protestant cemetery on Mount Zion in Jerusalem, but he donated his head to the Royal College of Surgeons in London for research.

William Foxwell Albright

By far the most influential person in the history of biblical or Levantine archaeology was William Foxwell Albright (1893–1971). Albright grew up in Chile where his parents served as

Methodist missionaries. He received his doctor of philosophy degree in ancient languages at age twenty-three from Johns Hopkins University, and he immediately began to influence the field of ancient Near Eastern archaeology. Albright's enormous intellect, strong biblical foundation, and tireless work ethic earned him the moniker, "the father of biblical archaeology." Albright published about eight hundred books, articles, and tracts, but his most influential work was *From the Stone Age to Christianity: Monotheism and the Historical Process.*[19]

The broader public became aware of Albright in the late 1940s and early 1950s when he authenticated the Dead Sea Scrolls. While teaching at Johns Hopkins University from 1929 to 1959, Albright continued to do exemplary fieldwork at sites such as Tell Beit Mirsim in the hill country of Israel. Tell Beit Mirsim was particularly important because the stratification represented all the archaeological ages, thus facilitating a refinement in the ceramic chronology. Even Albright's academic opponents recognized him as the world's leading expert on ceramics and linguistics.

Through the classroom and his fieldwork, Albright trained the next generation of Levantine archaeologists, thus ensuring his legacy. His protégé, G. Ernest Wright, continued his work. Albright's emphasis on interdisciplinary and regional thinking shines forth in the work of one of his star students, Nelson Glueck. Glueck surveyed the Transjordan region in the 1930s. Albright and Glueck freely assisted many excavations with their ceramic typology and oversight needs. For example, from 1926 to 1932, the Danish became the first to excavate at Shiloh. When their capable director, Hans Kjaer, suddenly died in the middle of the 1932 season, Glueck assumed the leadership reigns and quickly and smoothly ended the dig.

Although brilliant, Albright was sometimes narrow-minded. For example, he insisted that the Ai of Joshua 7–8 belonged at et-Tell, even after Joseph Callaway excavated the site in the 1960s and found no evidence of occupation during the time of the conquest. David Livingston engaged him on the issue, but Albright remained adamant. Albright wrote,

You can take it from me, and from Callaway and others, that there just isn't any other possibility for Ai than et-Tell and that Bethel can only have been modern Beitin. Since 1921 we have examined and reexamined the whole countryside, and there just isn't any archaeologically viable identification.[20]

Despite Albright's insistence, Livingston kept searching for viable candidates for Ai, and eventually settled on Khirbet Nisya, a site that he excavated from 1979 to 2002. While that site has potential, other archaeologists felt that there wasn't a strong enough correlation with the biblical requirements.

Yet another candidate for Ai entered the fray in 1994 when my ABR colleague, Bryant Wood, proposed Khirbet el-Maqatir, about a half mile southwest of et-Tell. Excavations there ran from 1995 to 2016, with the final three years under my direction. The site has emerged as the leading contender for the Ai of Joshua's time. Thus it seems that Albright's fixation on et-Tell got the better of him.[21]

Kathleen Kenyon

Kathleen Kenyon (1890–1978) ranks as another important person in the history of fieldwork. Kenyon was the daughter of the director of the British Museum. She graduated from Oxford University, and worked north of London under Mortimer Wheeler, from whom she learned the stratigraphic method.

Kenyon introduced to Palestinian archaeology her own version of Wheeler's method that involved trenching and the meticulous recording of data. Her vertical approach to excavation was widely adopted by modern archaeologists, but it has a drawback: relatively little architecture sees the light of day. Say, for example, that the corner of a temple appeared in the process of taking an excavation square down to bedrock. The Kenyon-Wheeler method would leave the remainder of the temple buried. By exposing only limited surface areas, there is a greater margin for interpretive error since the occupational history of one part of a tell can differ from another. Many archaeologists now combine careful vertical excavation with common-sense horizontal extensions, when needed. Emmanuel Eisenberg's work at Hebron exemplifies the combined approach.

Kenyon applied her methodology in extensive excavations at Tell es-Sultân (Jericho) from 1952 to 1958 and at Jerusalem from 1961 to 1967. At Jericho, she discovered evidence of human occupation that dated to the Neolithic period, thus establishing Jericho as one of the oldest cities in the world. Göbekli Tepe in Turkey now holds that distinction.[22] In Jerusalem, Kenyon excavated biblical Mount Zion, the oldest area of the city where David and Solomon established the headquarters of the united monarchy. Kenyon uncovered the famous *milô'* or Stepped Stone Structure (fig. 2.5). In 2005, Eilat Mazar proved that the *milô'* supported David's palace, the Large Stone Structure, now mostly excavated.[23]

Figure 2.5. Stepped Stone Structure

Despite Kenyon's many strengths, she lagged behind on the publication of her finds. While she did publish a popular work on Jericho in 1957 called *Digging Up Jericho*, and two massive volumes in 1960 and 1964, the overwhelming task of publishing the excavation material had to be tackled piecemeal alongside her other commitments. The final four volumes, which appeared posthumously between 1981 and 1983, were achieved only by the full-time employment of Thomas Holland as editor.

Kenyon lacked theological and linguistic training, but she excelled at field archaeology. She considered herself "unencumbered by any biblical baggage."[24] This probably explains her lack of precision in matching her archaeological definitions to the Bible. She concluded that Jericho sat unoccupied during the Late Bronze Age, the time of the biblical conquest. Bryant Wood, an expert in Late Bronze Age Canaanite pottery, disproved Kenyon's conclusions, siding with British archaeologist John Garstang, who excavated there in the 1930s. Kenyon neglected bichrome pottery and other important factors in her dating of Jericho.[25]

Yigael Yadin

In the middle of the twentieth century, Israeli archaeologists began to come out from under the shadows of their American and European mentors. One of the most prominent of the early Israeli archaeologists was Yigael Yadin (1917–1984) (fig. 2.6). He served as a soldier, scholar, politician, and archaeologist. Yadin and his father, Eleazar Sukenik, also an archaeologist, both played key

Figure 2.6. Yigael Yadin

roles in obtaining and translating the Dead Sea Scrolls. Moreover, in the caves near ʿEin-Gedi, Yadin also discovered correspondence relating to the Second Jewish Revolt against Rome.

Yadin excavated the huge site of Tell el-Qedah (Hazor) in northern Israel from 1955 to 1958 and again in 1968. He dug at Tell Megiddo, too. At both sites he uncovered and correctly identified the six-chambered Solomonic gate. Yadin also excavated at the desert fortress (Masada). His charismatic personality and political connections helped him recruit a large army of Israeli and American volunteers. This became a pattern for future excavations. Yadin's excavations became a type of field school for the next generation of Israeli archaeologists.

Kenneth Kitchen

Kenneth Kitchen, an elder statesman of ancient Near Eastern archaeology, ranks as the world's leading expert in Egyptian inscriptions. His book, *On the Reliability of the Old Testament*, stands at the forefront of contemporary scholarship. Kitchen crafted the well-known archaeological maxim, "absence of evidence is not evidence of absence." By this he meant that the presence of corroborating evidence can help establish the veracity of a text, but the lack of evidence cannot disprove a text's accuracy. Many factors could cause the disappearance or destruction of historical remains.

Shimon Gibson

Shimon Gibson represents all the best attributes in biblical archaeology. Born in Great Britain and raised in Jerusalem, Gibson

Figure 2.7. Shimon Gibson (*left*) and Scott Stripling (*right*) examining a figurine

began working on excavations in his early teenage years and graduated to supervisory roles by his late teens. A professor at the University of North Carolina at Charlotte, Gibson has excavated numerous sites in the Jerusalem area (fig. 2.7). Currently, he leads the dig at Mount Zion. Gibson tends to keep his faith commitments private, but there is no doubt about his commitment to non-biased archaeology. His book, *The Final Days of Jesus: The Archaeological Evidence*, masterfully reveals the real life setting of the week of passion, including the true path of the Via Dolorosa (the route of anguish).

The Minimalist Controversy

In contrast to Kitchen and Gibson, there is a small cadre of liberal archaeologists known as minimalists because of their disregard for the reliability of the biblical text. This group includes Niels Peter

Lemche, Thomas Thompson, and Philip Davies. Many scholars would also add to this revisionist group the prolific excavator and writer, Israel Finkelstein. The minimalists deny the historicity of the Old Testament narratives. From their perspective, the patriarchal narratives, the exodus, the conquest, and the united monarchy are all etiological or mythical legends. Their stance requires a radical reinterpretation of the established archaeological corpus.

For example, Finkelstein, currently excavating Tel Megiddo, dates the site's six-chambered gate to the ninth century, the time of Ahab. At that time, he says, Israel first built monumental architecture. In his view, a tenth-century construction could not have occurred because Solomon did not exist. Solomon did not exist because no evidence in the tenth century proves his existence. So goes the circular reasoning. To be fair, Finkelstein also argues his case on the basis of ceramics and other material remains.

Senior archaeologist William Dever, who is an enigma at times, points out the danger of the minimalist and deconstructionist paradigm:

> In the past decade or so, the deconstructionist mode of textual analysis—especially in the form of new literary criticism sketched above—has made such inroads in biblical studies that the traditional historical exegesis and criticism that have ruled for more than a century are often dismissed today as *passé*. If the search for "history" and for historical exegesis of texts is obsolete, the archaeology of the "biblical world" is irrelevant. That may explain why archaeology is neglected or at best misunderstood almost everywhere in biblical studies and theology today.[26]

The minimalists, following the various versions of the Documentary Hypothesis, believe that the Old Testament was written during the Hellenistic period or, at the earliest, during the time of Josiah (ca. 640–609 BC). Unfortunately, very few Bible-believing colleges and universities are training students in biblical archaeology or preparing them to refute the outlandish claims of the minimalists. However, not everyone has thrown in the towel—or the trowel. Some of the leading, biblically conservative institutions continue the work of Levantine archaeology. These institutions include the following:

- Andrews University. This institution has remained active the past thirty years through the Madaba Plains Excavation Project in Jordan. They currently dig at Tell Jalul.

- Associates for Biblical Research. The ABR team has excavated three sites in the highlands: Khirbet Nisya (1979–2002), Khirbet el-Maqatir (1995–2016), and Shiloh (2017–present).

- Averett University. In 2017, the university launched a new dig at Khirbet el-Mastereh, an Iron Age site in the Jordan Valley.

- Azusa Pacific University. Currently APU is excavating at Tel Abel Beth-Maacah in northern Israel.

- Liberty University. Representatives of Liberty work periodically in the cemetery and caves near Khirbet Qumran.

- Southern Adventist University. The SAU team participated in the excavation at Khirbet Qeiyafa (Elah fortress). They currently contribute to the consortium at Tel Lachish.

- Southwestern Baptist Theological Seminary. In the past, the seminary excavated at Timnah' and 'Azekah. Currently, they work at Gezer and on the island of Cyprus.

- Trinity Southwest University. Since 2005, TSU has been excavating at Tell el-Ḥammam in Jordan.

- Wheaton College. Until 2016, Wheaton participated in the consortium excavating at Ashkelon. The students continue to help in the survey of Tel Shimron.

Other faith-based institutions such as William Jessup University and Gordon-Conwell Theological Seminary maintain archaeology programs. Archaeology classes are offered at Lee University, Assemblies of God Theological Seminary, The Bible Seminary, Southwest Baptist University, the University of Northwestern at St. Paul, and the University of Pikeville.

The New Archaeology

In recent decades, archaeology has become more specialized and interdisciplinary in nature. This is sometimes referred to as processualism, a form of archaeology that considers the impact of environment, culture, and lifestyle. It involves more of a comprehensive, anthropological, and regional approach to site interpretation. A dig director manages a staff of experts and volunteers. In addition to the core field staff, experts and specialists serve on retainer. Epigraphists interpret inscriptions; entomologists identify insects; geologists categorize rocks; and numismatists study coins. The list goes on. The new archaeology employs a sociological and anthropological approach—it not only reveals how the elite of a society lived, but it also seeks to understand the daily life of common people. Walter Rast and Thomas Shaub excavated Bab edh-Dhra' and Numeira on the southeastern shore of the Dead Sea from 1973 to 1979. Rast writes,

> During excavation, evidence frequently comes to light showing how people arranged their dwellings. Within the houses themselves data may indicate how areas were used—whether for food preparation, storage, or for keeping animals. Some buildings undoubtedly had special purposes, such as for pottery making or flint-knapping. Room and house size can also indicate average numbers of people in a family, or the status of the family itself.[27]

A few seasons of fieldwork can now occupy scholars for decades. Today's archaeologist thinks regionally, endeavoring to determine how his or her site illuminates the findings at other sites, and vice versa. For example, the absence of Late Bronze Age pottery at one site merits notice, but when combined with the same gap at nearby sites, it becomes an instructive pattern.

While the newer, interdisciplinary approach and the improved technology of the last decades have no doubt produced better and more reliable data, they have also made archaeology an expensive discipline. The average excavation season of four weeks now exceeds $250,000 in expenses. It sometimes takes years to secure this level of funding. Eilat Mazar from Hebrew University expressed confidence that she knew the location of David's palace in Jerusalem, but a decade passed before she could raise the funds for excavation.

Most modern archaeologists attempt to interpret the physical remains from a systems theory perspective. Systems theory emphasizes the impact on multiple aspects of a site or culture when one aspect is changed. For example, the invention of pottery in the middle of the Neolithic Age radically impacted other aspects of the Neolithic culture such as trade, food storage, cultic practice, and food preparation.

In the ABR excavation at Shiloh which I direct, supervisors use iPad devices in the field to record data, which is automatically integrated into our database. While we still manually section and draw some of our pottery, most of it runs through high-tech scanners at Hebrew University that produce perfect drawings within seconds. We also implemented the new technology of wet sifting. After excavated material is dry sifted, it goes through the wet sift in order to ensure that not even the smallest piece of evidence is missed. At the same time, water is added to the soil so that seeds will float to the surface and can be saved for analysis. A botanist analyzes the seeds, and a zooarchaeologist analyzes the faunal remains. Together, this data reveals the diet of the ancient inhabitants. At Shiloh, metal detectors probe every locus of every excavation square. Specialists conduct neutron activation analysis, carbon dating, and other scientific tests. All of these specialized activities require money.

Dating Methods in Archaeology

Archaeologists must be able to accurately date the remains that they excavate in order to determine the stratification of the site. To do this, they employ several methods.

Dating by Historical Synchronisms

Fixed dates in the Bible can be used to determine the dates of archaeological remains. For example, the Babylonians destroyed Jerusalem in 587 BC; therefore, it would not be hard to date an Iron Age IIC destruction level at Jerusalem or Tel Lachish to 587 BC.[28] Another fixed date is the construction of Solomon's Temple in 966 BC. Even David Rohl and the proponents of the so-called new chronology would not challenge this date, though they would not assign it to Iron Age IIA as most scholars do.

The Egyptian and Mesopotamian dynasties maintained extensive records and elaborate chronologies. They often made direct or indirect references to biblical characters or events. For example, the Merenptah relief in Egypt refers to Israel as an established people group in the Levant in the second year of Merenptah's reign (ca. 1209 BC). The dating harmonizes with the viewpoint that Israel had already been settled in the land for two centuries.

A few centuries later, Elisha anointed Jehu as Israel's king. Jehu was forced to pay tribute to the powerful Assyrian king, Shalmaneser III. The Black Obelisk of Shalmaneser III confirms this fact. The fixed date of 825 BC confirms the date of the obelisk.

Dating by Pottery

In the 1890s, Flinders Petrie used various pottery forms to determine the date of material remains in a given stratum. Albright, Glueck, and Kenyon further demonstrated the validity of dating based on ceramic typology. Ceramic dating remains the most important and most accurate means of dating in the field of archaeology. For example, the red-slipped burnished pottery found in the six-chambered gate at Gezer helped date the gate to the time of Solomon. Burnishing is the process of rubbing the painted surface of the pottery with a bone or rock so that it takes on a shiny finish. Moreover, the size of the inclusions in Iron Age I pottery betrays its ceramic sequence. Rims evert in one age and invert in the next age. Dozens of such diagnostic features yield accurate dates based on pottery. Diagnostic sherds include pieces of rims, handles, bases, painted pieces, or inscribed (glyptic) pieces.

Dating by Carbon-14

Carbon-14 dating, originally discovered by Willard Libby, measures the breakdown of radioactive isotopes within organic material. These isotopes break down at a predictable rate, thus allowing scientists to accurately determine the age of an object. The C-14 ratio in the atmosphere fluctuates due to solar activity, atomic explosions, large volcanic eruptions, shifts in the earth's magnetic field, and other factors. Practitioners assume that the ratio of C-14 in the past was the same as it is today.

Carbon-14 dating is normally accurate to within fifty years, but the further back in time that archaeologists probe, the more necessary it becomes to calibrate dates using other means, such as dendrochronology. A debate rages at Tel Megiddo regarding the date of certain architectural features, such as Solomon's stables. Voices from both sides of the debate attempt to use C-14 to establish their chronology, but the dispute continues because of the fifty-year margin of error. Carbon dating is expensive, so archaeologists use it sparingly.

At Khirbet el-Maqatir, my team uncovered eight human skeletons in an elaborate subterranean hiding system (fig. 2.8). Our anthropologist extracted collagen samples from the bones for C-14

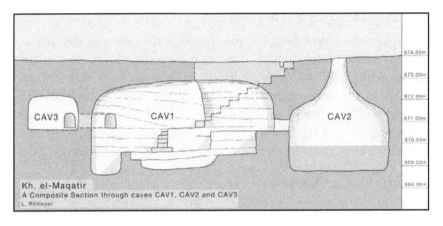

Figure 2.8. Subterranean system at Khirbet el-Maqatir

testing. The results showed that the skeletons dated to the mid-first-century AD. This date matched the ceramic and numismatic dates that we had tentatively reached.

Dating by Numismatics

Numismatics is the study of coins. Coins first came into use in the Persian period, around 550 BC. Numismatists can date most coins to within a few years of their origin; therefore, coins are a valuable tool in the establishing of chronology, given that they come from a clean or sealed locus. A coin of Archelaus, who reigned in Judea and Samaria from only 4 BC to AD 6, can be used to date the stratum in which it was found. At Khirbet el-Maqatir, we recovered almost fourteen hundred coins. Bronze coins dominate the numismatic corpus, with only five silver coins and two gold coins.

Procedures in Field Archaeology

So, how does one go about excavating an archaeological site? First, a qualified archaeologist must secure a license to excavate. In Israel, the Israel Antiquities Authority or one of its subsidiaries regulates all excavations. In Jordan, the Department of Antiquities governs all matters archaeological. At times, sites are on private property owned by multiple parties, and this requires a second set of negotiations and contracts. In order to obtain permits, one must perform initial research, such as surveying, collecting surface sherds, and so forth. One must also write proposals and do a fair amount of diplomatic schmoozing.

Second, money must be raised. Sometimes this can be a protracted process requiring additional written proposals as well as developed procurement skills. Some archaeologists look to university budgets or endowments; others approach foundations; still others solicit the broader public directly. As mentioned, Eilat Mazar, who excavated King David's palace, sought funding for a decade before finding a benefactor for her project.

Third, a team must assemble. This normally involves the dig director, assistant directors, square supervisors, volunteers, local workers, and specialists. Most team members work as uncompensated volunteers. Sometimes the senior staff is compensated, but other times everyone works for free. Specialists such as geologists and paleobotanists are usually kept on retainer and only called on if needed. Once assembled, the team receives a site-specific orientation and training.

Fourth, protocols must be established. One must decide how the data will be collected, recorded, and published. At Shiloh, we use the protocols in the excavation manual of the Madaba Plains Project, with some adaptations.[29]

Fifth, the administrative details must be implemented. Where will the group lodge? How will the group be transported daily? Where will artifacts be stored? How will sensitive equipment get in and out of the country? How will the language barriers be overcome?

Sixth, a surveyor must establish a grid with fixed longitude, latitude, and GPS coordinates. The grid consists of excavation squares that must be plotted. Some excavators prefer squares that are six-by-six meters (about eighteen-by-eighteen feet), while other excavators favor squares that are five-by-five meters (about fifteen-by-fifteen feet). A portion of the square often remains unexcavated and functions as a balk (fig. 2.9). Dig directors usually opt to leave balks on the north and east sides of the square

Figure 2.9. Studying the balk

in order to preserve the stratigraphy that existed prior to excavation. So in effect, the excavated square measures five-by-five meters, or four-by-four meters (about twelve-by-twelve feet), unless it is further sub-balked. Some dig directors leave a three-foot balk on all four sides initially. Balks are often removed at a later date. During excavation, they can make it easier to traverse the site without walking through areas of active excavation.

Seventh, the actual excavation begins. First comes the removal of the topsoil, along with any loose debris. This becomes "Locus 1" within that specified square and field. Workers gently trowel back or lightly pick through the earth as they descend in a uniform manner. Holes are never dug because they can destroy stratigraphy. The team removes dirt and debris from the square, while placing any pottery or artifacts in the appropriate locus pail. Before important objects are removed, they are photographed and measured for elevation, relative to sea level. Changes of the soil, pottery, or artifacts can indicate the emergence of a new occupational phase and provide a rationale for a new locus. As the square gets deeper, elevations must be recorded, drawings created, and photographs taken. The square supervisor communicates with the field director regarding the progress, and the field director likewise consults with the dig director when appropriate.

After the digging, members of the team wash and record the pottery and the objects. Only a small percentage of the finds reach the publication phase. Whole vessels are always published, along with choice diagnostic sherds. The post-excavation analysis team further studies the publishable materials in order to confirm or correct the findings in the field. For example, the team might initially determine that a rim dates to the Iron Age, but later conclude that it came from the Middle Bronze Age. The best of the publishable pieces may ultimately go on display at a museum in the host country or at the excavation's sponsoring institution.

Finally, the senior staff members write the final season reports and begin preparations for the next season. A season normally lasts three to six weeks. In the off-season, senior staff write preliminary dig reports for peer-reviewed and popular journals, and they present papers at academic conferences. After several seasons of excavation, the staff usually begin to draft the final publication, which can fill multiple volumes.

Further Study and Discussion

How does the work of a field archaeologist differ from the image of an archaeologist as portrayed by Hollywood (e.g., Indiana Jones and Lara Croft)?

What presuppositions distinguish the minimalists? Why should Christian leaders be aware of these presuppositions?

In what ways did W. F. Albright benefit from being raised by missionary parents in Chile?

What new technologies improve the excavation practices of archaeologists?

Absence of evidence is not evidence of absence.

❖ Kenneth Kitchen

Chapter 3

The Pre-patriarchal and Patriarchal Ages

The events of Genesis 1–11 that precede Abraham find many parallels in the mythology of the ancient Near East.[30] Important examples from Mesopotamia include a flood story known as the Gilgamesh Epic and a creation epic known as the Enuma Elish (fig. 3.1). Both epics have numerous similarities and differences with the biblical account.

In the currently accepted chronology, the events prior to the Tower of Babel divide into four periods: the Neolithic Age, the Chalcolithic Age, the Early Bronze Age, and the Intermediate Bronze Age. A familiarity with these eras facilitates understanding and interpretation of the earliest archaeological strata.

Figure 3.1. Enuma Elish fragment

The Neolithic Age

Figure 3.2. Tower at Jericho, Neolithic Age

The Neolithic Age (10,000–4500 BC?) refers to the time when people first began to shift from a nomadic lifestyle to a semi-nomadic lifestyle. During this Neolithic revolution, people harvested grains such as wheat and barley, and they raised animals such as sheep and goats. Importantly, they discovered pottery, which accelerated the development of civilization. Tell es-Sultân (Jericho) and ʿAin Ghazal (near Amman) exhibit the classic transition from pre-pottery cultures to pottery cultures (cf. fig. 3.2). We have ample evidence of trade between regions in the Neolithic Age. For example, Neolithic sites across the Levant contain obsidian (black volcanic glass) from Turkey and bitumen from the Dead Sea.

Burials were often underneath the floors of domestic structures. Round houses and circular villages characterized the Neolithic era. Fertility rites formed the basis of religion, as evidenced by the figurines of females with exaggerated hips and breasts. The figurines likely served as a type of talisman (good luck charm).

Since 1995, the amazing Neolithic site of Göbekli Tepe in southeastern Anatolia (modern Turkey) has been under excavation by a German team led by Klaus Schmidt. More than a dozen circles, formed from T-shaped megaliths, have emerged. Many of the T-shaped megaliths display intricate carvings of animals. No potsherds have surfaced, so it can confidently be assigned to the pre-pottery Neolithic period, or PPN for short. There are two further subdivisions of the PPN period. The excavators refer to the earlier phase of occupation as PPNA, and the later phase as PPNB. The site underwent an apparent intentional burial, perhaps reflecting the residents' hope of eventual return. Another PPN site was recently discovered at Motza, west of Jerusalem. It is a salvage excavation required for highway expansion.

The Chalcolithic Age

The Chalcolithic Age (4500–3200 BC?) saw the emergence of more homogeneous cultures and larger settlements. Humans discovered copper technology in this era, and from this discovery the era draws its name. Major Chalcolithic centers existed at Teleilat el-Ghassul, near the Yarmuk River, and in the Golan Heights. Chalcolithic peoples built subterranean rooms and even dammed nearby wadis in order to create water reserves. Many people traded freely with villagers and continued to live in rural or pastoral areas. The transition from the Chalcolithic Age to the Early Bronze Age occurred gradually, as evidenced by the basalt bowls found in the shaft tombs at Bab edh-Dhraʿ. These tombs revealed the continued practice of secondary burial in the Early Bronze I period, although their Chalcolithic ancestors preferred clay ossuaries rather than shaft tombs. The pottery types also continued for the most part.

The Dead Sea region witnessed the ubiquitous production of copper objects in the Late Chalcolithic Age, as seen in the Cave of Treasures. On the other hand, the Early Bronze IA strata reveal no awareness of metallurgy. The reappearance of copper objects in the Early Bronze IB period indicates a cultural regression at the end of the Chalcolithic Age. Class structures likely first began to develop in this era. Most sites at the end of the Chalcolithic Age show evidence of abandonment, not destruction, perhaps due to a reduction in rainfall levels.

Figure 3.3. Temple at ʿEin-Gedi, Chalcolithic Age

A large Chalcolithic temple sits atop the cliffs of ʿEin-Gedi, overlooking the Dead Sea (fig. 3.3). Flint is extremely common at Chalcolithic sites. It served an important utilitarian role even though the people possessed ceramic and copper objects.

The Early Bronze Age

The invention of bronze and an increase in annual precipitation brought about a new era. Bronze comes from the smelting of copper and tin. It produces a stronger metal than copper alone. The Early Bronze Age, known as the first age of cities, began about 3200 BC. A few centuries later, the ancient Near East underwent an urban transition from villages to cities. This transition permanently changed life in the eastern Mediterranean world.

Cities were, of course, small by modern standards, but in Mesopotamia, Uruk grew to four hundred acres, and in Egypt, some sites were nearly as large. The process of urbanization materialized at Tell el-Ḥammam where the city spread to over one hundred acres. The possibility exists that the large and advanced Ghassulian culture (just a few miles away) relocated to Tell el-Ḥammam after the unexplained abandonment at Teleilat el-Ghassul. Arad is one of the best-known Early Bronze Age cities. It had a six-foot-wide city wall with defensive towers. Pottery at Arad reveals extensive trade with other regions. One example is an ostracon referring to Narmer, Egypt's first pharaoh.[31]

Pottery continued to be handmade until late in the Early Bronze I period when the potter's slow wheel seems to come into use. The slow wheel allowed the potter to shape the vessel with one hand while turning the wheel with the other. Because of the slow wheel, a proliferation of types appear in the archaeological record. The most famous types include (a) line-group painted ceramics, which have a series of vertical lines with dark paint, and (b) Khirbet Kerak ware, which has a burnished black exterior (fig. 3.4). Khirbet Kerak sits on the southern shore of the Sea of Galilee. This pottery is particularly diagnostic because of its absence from strata before and after the Early Bronze III period. Hence, an Early Bronze Age stratum can often be accurately dated based on the presence or absence of Khirbet Kerak ware.

Rarely in human history has there been such a widespread breakdown of a civilization as what occurred

Figure 3.4. Khirbet Kerak ware

at the end of the Early Bronze Age. Most scholars agree that a reduction of rainfall caused many settled people groups to return to their formerly nomadic or semi-nomadic ways of life.[32] Humans also impacted their surrounding environment. It appears that the inhabitants of sites such as Jericho and Bab edh-Dhra' cut down the local forests for the construction of their cities. The deforestation left the surrounding area denuded and likely lowered the water table. The lowering of the water table coupled with the reduction in rainfall was more than the large Early Bronze Age cities could withstand. The period ended around 2350 BC with the mysterious abandonment of the large fortified cities across the Levant.

The Intermediate Bronze Age

The entire urban system began to collapse at the end of the Early Bronze III period. It is probably the greatest such crash in antiquity, and it occurred over the span of a century. The Mari texts from coastal Syria refer to an invasion of nomadic people that certainly destabilized the region. Nevertheless, a few sites were partially rebuilt, and even a few new sites were established from about 2350 BC to 1950 BC, a period often referred to as the Intermediate Bronze Age.[33] Paleobotanists have concluded that during the third millennium BC, people first cultivated grapes and olives, thus creating important industries for the region.

Tell Iktanu, excavated in the 1990s by Kay Pragg on behalf of the University of Manchester, yielded evidence of occupation throughout the Intermediate Bronze Age, but it suffered permanent abandonment around 1950 BC.[34] Khirbet Iskander and Beer Resisim also had significant cities during this era. Sites with their own springs continued to thrive during the Intermediate Bronze Age. East of the Jordan, Tell el-Ḥammam provides a good example, and west of the Jordan Jericho shows signs of unbroken occupation.

Around 1950 BC, rainfall levels increased slightly, ending a fifty year drought, like the one referred to in Genesis. And nomads began to rebuild many of the Early Bronze Age sites. The construction boom brought about the Middle Bronze Age (1950–1483 BC), known as the second age of cities. Generally speaking, re-urbanization began near the Mediterranean Sea and gradually spread eastward.

The Patriarchs

The patriarchs—Abraham, Isaac, and Jacob—belong to the Intermediate Bronze Age culture. Abraham lived around 2100 BC.[35] Because the patriarchs were nomads, few archaeological remains verify their existence. Abraham's tent and Jacob's pillar have long since perished or been lost. However, the tombs of the patriarchs in Hebron provides a direct connection with the patriarchs. Abraham purchased the cave of Machpelah as a burial site for his wife Sarah (Gen 15:18). And later, Machpelah became the burial site for Abraham, Isaac, and Jacob (15:9–10; 35:27–29; 49:29–32; 50:13). In the first century BC, Herod the Great built a huge enclosure over the tombs. The enclosure remains intact even today. Not surprisingly, it looks like a miniature Temple Mount platform. Jews, Muslims, and Christians venerate the site, and nowadays, this results in conflicts—conflicts like the 1992 massacre. Today, heavy security protects the entrances to the temenos.

Many cultural clues from the Intermediate Bronze Age confirm the ancestral narrative of Genesis and reveal its authenticity. The covenant language of Genesis 15, for example, would not have been employed in earlier or later time periods. The Mosaic covenant of the Late Bronze Age resembles the five-point model of the Hittite suzerain treaties. Writers of each age structured their covenants in a unique manner just like potters of each era created different forms and used different styles. Of course, there were differences between the treaty forms as well. Furthermore, the household gods (Hebrew: *tərāpîm*) that Rachel stole from her father Laban reflect the material culture of the Immediate Bronze Age. These terra-cotta figurines, only four to eight inches tall, were unique to the Intermediate and Middle Bronze Ages.

The Cities of the Plain

The ancestral narrative records the destruction of Sodom, Gomorrah, and the other cities of the plain. Many researchers have proposed identifications for these infamous cities. In the 1930s, Albright popularized the notion that Sodom might be found at the southern end of the Dead Sea, or beneath the waters of the southern end.

The cities of Bab edh-Dhra' and Numeira have garnered much attention as candidates for Sodom and Gomorrah because they were destroyed by a fiery conflagration in the distant past. But these identifications face serious chronological and geographical challenges.

Concerning the chronology, the excavators initially reported a destruction date around 2350 BC, but they later amended their conclusion and said that Numeira met its demise 250 years earlier. Even if both sites were destroyed around 2350 BC, that is still two hundred years too early to fit the earliest permissible interpretation of the Masoretic Text. The Septuagint offers a date around 1820 BC for the destruction of Sodom and Gomorrah.[36] Judges 11:26, 1 Kings 6:1, and Exodus 12:40 provide the basis for dating the events described in Genesis (table 3.1).

Table 3.1. Timeline of the Old Testament

2166	Abraham born
1876	Jacob in Egypt
1526	Moses born
1446	Exodus
1399	Tabernacle at Shiloh
1200	Deborah
1040	David born
966	Solomon's Temple
723	Assyrian captivity
587	Solomon's Temple destroyed
483	Esther saves Jews
432	Nehemiah and Malachi

In addition to the chronological problems problems complicate the identification of Bab Numeira as Sodom and Gomorrah. Genesis 13:1–' of the parting of Abram and Lot. As they stood between _ Ai, Lot gazed upon the whole plain of the Jordan, including the cities of the plain. He then moved eastward and pitched his tents "near" (or "as far as") Sodom. Wherever Sodom was located, Lot must have been able to see it while standing between Bethel and Ai. From 2010 to 2017, I spent hundreds of days at this spot while working at Khirbet el-Maqatir. In my view, anything past the northern edge of the Dead Sea should be eliminated from consideration.

In 2005, Steven Collins launched the Tell el-Ḥammam excavation. He argues that Sodom was located there, Gomorrah at Tell Kefrein, Admah at Tell Nimrin, and the Zeboiim at Tells Bleibel and Mustah. The location north of the Dead Sea works well with the geographical description of Genesis 13, and the large and impressive site did suffer a massive destruction in the Bronze Age. Problematically, the ceramic dating at Tell el-Ḥammam points to a destruction around 1650 BC. That is 400 years too late for the Masoretic Text date, and about 170 years too late for the Septuagint date. To compensate for the shortfall, Collins, who originally embraced the Septuagint reading, now holds to a more elastic dating system based on honorific numbers. Perhaps the evidence that Collins seeks resides in the Intermediate Bronze Age strata at Tell el-Ḥammam.[37]

Many scholars fervently believe that Bab edh-Dhra' and Numeira are Sodom and Gomorrah. Others believe with equal fervency that the infamous sin cities existed at Tell el-Ḥammam and Tell Kefrein. For now, the location of the cities of the plain remains a mystery.

Further Study and Discussion

What role did climate change play in ancient civilizations?

What caused the Neolithic revolution, and how does it compare to modern western civilization?

How did metallurgy affect ancient people groups?

What was the first great age of cities? Does this possibly correspond to the Tower of Babel?

If we excavate a site and do not publish the results,
we have destroyed the evidence and made it
inaccessible to others.

❖ Jodi Magness

Chapter 4

The Middle Bronze Age

The Middle Bronze Age traditionally dates from 1950 BC to 1483 BC. This period is known for the development of cities in Canaan and the role of the Hyksos. Various cultural characteristics distinguish the Middle Bronze Age.

Cultural Characteristics

General prosperity marks the Middle Bronze period. Local economies flourished, and trade prospered on both sides of the Jordan. Let us take a closer look at the cultural milieu, namely, the domestic implements, the fortification practices, the burial traditions, and the religious beliefs. The Middle Bronze period even furnishes some evidence of literary activity.

Domestic Implements

Early in the Middle Bronze era, potters developed the fast wheel or kick wheel. This new technology freed both hands of the potter to work his vessel, and as a result, pottery forms proliferated. Potters also discovered the process of levigation, whereby clay was soaked in water in order to remove impurities such as small stones. Generally speaking, handles were elongated and rims everted (tilted outward). Carination on bowls and goblets was also introduced. The single-spout lamp first appeared in this period, and it continued with refinement to the Early Roman Age. Potters certainly excelled at their craft in the Middle Bronze Age (fig. 4.1).

Flint continued in wide usage throughout the Middle Bronze Age. The most notable utilitarian tool was the sickle blade, a series of knapped flints with serrated blades that are wedged into the groove of a wooden sickle. Urban winepresses likely existed at many Middle Bronze Age sites in Canaan, but the first example of urban wine production only came to light in 2016 at Tel Kabri.

Figure 4.1. Chocolate-on-white storage jar, Middle Bronze Age

Fortification Practices

Improved environmental and social conditions proved favorable for the resettlement of cities. Thus, the Middle Bronze Age is also known as the second age of cities. Many Early Bronze Age cities finally underwent reconstruction, but some, like et-Tell, remained in ruins, perhaps because the water sources could not be reestablished. The recovery of cities happened first on the west side of the Jordan, beginning in the coastal plain, and then later spread to many sites on the east side. Large city-states thrived and controlled numerous satellite towns. Nomadic pastoralists lived on the fringe of urban centers, creating a sort of symbiotic relationship with the city dwellers. The large and fortified cities of the Middle Bronze Age still appeared diminutive when juxtaposed to their Early Bronze Age predecessors.

City builders laid out the urban centers in orthogonal patterns. Typically, they erected large ramparts around the perimeter of a city and constructed the city wall on top of the ramparts. This had the effect of creating a glacis or slope around the city. A glacis made it extremely difficult for invaders to approach the city with momentum, and it neutralized offensive siege devices such as battering rams. I have seen several volunteers take bad falls when trying to scale a glacis slowly, so it is hard to imagine warriors ascending at full speed. Almost every Middle Bronze Age city in the Levant had a glacis, such as the one excavated at Gezer from the Middle Bronze III period.

Figure 4.2. Glacis at Ashkelon, Middle Bronze Age

Shiloh, Shechem, and Khirbet el-Maqatir also witnessed the construction of cyclopean size fortification systems in the Middle Bronze III period; whereas Jerusalem was fortified earlier in Middle Bronze II. Shechem (Tell Balaṭah) initially benefited from fortification in the Middle Bronze I, as did Tell el-Ḥammam.[38] The Middle Bronze II glacis and gate complex at Ashkelon offer tourists an impressive view of an ancient fortification system (fig. 4.2). Excavations also revealed heavy fortification at Aphek, by the mouth of the Yarkon River.

Builders in the Middle Bronze Age favored megaliths in their monumental construction. Good examples come from Hazor, west of the Jordan, and Pella to the east.

Residents entered cities through the gate complex, which normally had several chambers or phases. Gates in the Middle Bronze Age were large and sometimes arched and made of plastered mud-brick. Beautifully preserved examples have been excavated and conserved at Dan and Ashkelon (fig. 4.3). Some gates, like the one at Shechem, boasted massive orthostats in the

Figure 4.3. Gate at Tell Dan, Middle Bronze Age

entry. The leaders of a city often meted out justice and consummated business transactions in the city gate. Genesis 19:1 indicates that when the angelic messengers arrived, Lot was sitting in the gate of Sodom, apparently in a position of leadership.

Burial Traditions

Parents in the Middle Bronze Age typically buried their deceased infants in large clay jars, placed below the floor of their domestic dwellings. Ta'anach and Khirbet el-Maqatir yield classic examples of these infant jar burials. People buried their deceased friends and relatives in caves with elaborate ceremonies and expensive burial goods, such as weapons, pottery vessels, and scarabs. Multiple generations often shared common burial caves which were entered via a shaft. With rare exceptions, such as Beit Shean and Gibeon, the caves had only one chamber. Sometimes animals were sacrificed at the entrance of the tombs of the elite. The dog cemetery at Ashkelon provides evidence of animal sacrifices in the Middle Bronze era.

Religious Beliefs

Polytheistic religions continued to center on fertility rites as well as nature gods and goddesses, except among the few monotheists represented by Abraham's descendants. The god El led the Canaanite pantheon, along with his wife Asherah and his son Baal. Canaanite mythology resembles Greek (Aegean) mythology in many ways. It remains uncertain which culture influenced the other culture, or for that matter, if the influence was mutual. At Gezer, the excavators discovered a temple and "standing stones" (Hebrew: maṣēbôt), reflecting the religion of those who lived there.

Literary Activity

In 2017, my ABR colleague, Douglas Petrovich, released his groundbreaking research on ancient alphabetic script. His book demonstrates that Hebrew was the world's first alphabetic script.[39] Hebeded's use of proto-consonantal B in the caption on Sinai 115 at Serabit el-Khadim, which dates to year eighteen of Amenemhat III, represents the first sign of the alphabet. It dates to approximately 1842 BC. Sinai 377, the first complete proto-consonantal Hebrew inscription, dates to just two years later. This four-letter inscription comes from the Wadi Nasb, which served as

Serabit's source for water during mining campaigns. Both sites are in southwest-central Sinai.

The Hyksos Period

The Hyksos, conquerors from Canaan, ruled Lower Egypt during the Second Intermediate Period (ca. 1786–1570 BC). The unnamed pharaoh in Exodus 1:8 who "did not know Joseph" was likely the first Hyksos king. As a Canaanite, he would have been unaware of Joseph's status and accomplishments in the distant past. The Asiatic Hyksos imposed their might upon Egypt in the mid-seventeenth century BC and dominated the native inhabitants for 108 years, according to the Turin King List. They likely feared an Israelite confederacy with the Egyptians. Thus, the Hyksos placed the Israelites in bondage, forcing the slaves to construct major commercial centers at Pithom and Rameses, later names by which these places became known. Later copyists likely updated the names, thus creating an unfortunate anachronism. Updating place names commonly occurred in antiquity (e.g., Jebus became Jerusalem).

The Egyptians expelled the Hyksos in the mid-sixteenth century BC under the leadership of Ahmose, the founder of the Eighteenth Dynasty. The expulsion of the Hyksos provides the milieu of Exodus 1:13. Pithom likely corresponds to Tell el-Maskhuta, which

Figure 4.4. Scarab from Khirbet el-Maqatir, Hyksos period

John Holladay Jr. of the University of Toronto excavated from 1978 to 1985. Manfred Bietak's excavations over several decades at Tell ed-Dab'a (ancient Avaris) demonstrate a connection with the store city of Rameses. Avaris functioned as an important administrative center for the Hyksos, and the name changed to Rameses during the Twelfth Dynasty. Bietak uncovered pottery and a four-room house indicative of an Israelite presence at the site. A monumental tomb for an Asiatic dignitary possibly belonged to Joseph.

The Hyksos hegemony clearly extended to Canaanite and Amorite sites as scarabs such as the one from Khirbet el-Maqatir appear at numerous sites throughout Israel (fig. 4.4). When excavated in sealed loci, scarabs provide strong evidence for accurate stratigraphical dating.

The End of the Middle Bronze Age

People abandoned cities at the close of the Early Bronze Age. But in the late Middle Bronze Age, marauders destroyed cities, or the cities imploded because of social or political factors. The expulsion of the Hyksos from Egypt may have also brought tremendous demographic pressure to bear on the Canaanite city-states of the Levant. The transition between periods always occurs somewhat fluidly. In other words, the Middle Bronze Age did not end sharply in the year 1550. In fact, it was almost a century later that Pharaoh Thutmose III destroyed many of the Canaanite cities of the Middle Bronze Age. The relief from the Karnak temple portrays Thutmose III smiting a Syro-Palestinian prisoner (fig. 4.5). Narmer, Egypt's first pharaoh, took a similar pose with his enemies centuries earlier. The pharaoh holds the prisoners by their hair with their hands raised in the air as they beg for mercy.

With the end of the Middle Bronze Age around 1483 BC, the entire Levant entered a major cultural decline known as the Late Bronze Age. The next chapter explores this interesting and controversial time period.

Figure 4.5. Pylon of Thutmose III smiting prisoners, Karnak temple

Further Study and Discussion

Why did the population and the size of cities decrease after the Early Bronze Age and again after the Middle Bronze Age?

Why is the Middle Bronze Age known as the second age of cities?

Who were the Hyksos, and why were they important?

How did the invention of the potter's fast wheel influence pottery manufacturing?

The one who first states a case seems right,
until the other comes and cross-examines.

❖ Proverbs 18:17

Chapter 5

The Late Bronze Age

The Late Bronze Age spans about 350 years, from 1483 BC to 1177 BC. This period covers the exodus from Egypt, the wilderness wanderings, and the conquest and settlement of Canaan. Just as the Middle Bronze Age cities were smaller than their Early Bronze Age predecessors, so Late Bronze Age cities were considerably smaller than the Middle Bronze Age cities. In fact, the population of the Levant at this time declined by about 75 percent from a thousand years earlier. The walled cities of Jericho and Jebus (later Jerusalem) encompass- ed merely ten acres in size, and the largest city, Hazor, covered only one hundred acres. The poorly made pottery, inferior to the preceding eras, reflects the widespread cultural decline of the Late Bronze Age. Some notable vessels include bichrome ware and chocolate-on-white ware (fig. 5.1). The latter was a carryover style from the Middle Bronze Age.

Figure 5.1. Chocolate-on-white jug, Late Bronze Age

The Date of the Exodus

Israel's exodus from Egypt can be dated internally from the biblical text. First Kings 6:1 indicates that the exodus occurred either 479 or 439 years before Solomon began to build the temple in Jerusalem. The Masoretic Text reads 480, while the Septuagint reads 440. Solomon built the temple in 966 BC; therefore, the exodus occurred in the fifteenth century BC. Judges 11:26 also supports the fifteenth-century date of the exodus. Jephthah (ca. 1100 BC) informed the king of Amman that the Israelites had already been in the land for three hundred years.

Many scholars have tried to place the exodus in the reign of Ramesses II, around 1250 BC, but this requires a reinterpretation of the internal biblical chronology. The pharaoh of the exodus was not Ramesses II, but a pharaoh of the Eighteenth Egyptian Dynasty in the fifteenth century BC.[40] A strong case can be made for Amenhotep II, but researchers posit plausible arguments for a number of the pharaohs who preceded and succeeded him.

Interpreters who support a late date for the exodus often claim an absence of occupational evidence at a given site when the Bible indicates that the Israelites conquered it. The sage reader must bear in mind that such advocates refer to the evidence at the end of the Late Bronze Age, rather than the middle of the Late Bronze Age. *Those looking at the wrong time period for evidence of the conquest are certain to not find any.* Authors such as William Dever argue forcefully that no one occupied the northern Negev or Jericho in the Late Bronze Age. However, only a small percentage of tells, such as Arad and Beersheba, have been excavated. And others tells, such as Edrei, are beneath modern cities, and therefore inaccessible to archaeologists. Numbers 21:1–3 relates that the Israelites conquered Arad, yet excavations at the assumed location revealed an occupational gap at the time of the biblical conquest. However, in Pharaoh Shishak's tenth-century campaign, he mentions two Arads, one of which remains unknown. Apparently, the biblical text refers to this second Arad.

Scarcity of population must also be understood in light of the generally recognized view that many of the Late Bronze Age inhabitants of the Levant reverted to nomadic or semi-nomadic lifestyles. Such lifestyles do not leave an imprint in the archaeological record. Time and again further excavation proves the arguments of the skeptics to be lacking in credibility.

Dever typifies the problem of abandoning biblical chronology when he writes of Jericho:

> Kenyon, however, equipped with far superior modern methods, and proclaiming herself unencumbered by any "biblical baggage" (so she once told me in Jerusalem), proved that while this destruction indeed dated to *ca.* 1500 B.C., it was part of the well-attested Egyptian campaigns in the course of expelling the Asiatic "Hyksos" from Egypt at the beginning of the 18th Dynasty. Moreover, Kenyon showed beyond doubt that in the mid-late 13th century B.C. — the time period now required for any Israelite "conquest" — Jericho lay completely abandoned. There is not so much as a Late Bronze II potsherd of that period on the entire site.[41]

On one hand, Dever recognizes the probability of a fifteenth-century BC destruction at Jericho, which he conveniently chooses to attribute to Egyptians rather than Israelites. On the other hand, he "proves" there was no conquest at Jericho because there was no destruction there around 1200 BC. Presuppositions can control even the most eminent scholars. In fact, Dever spends two chapters of his book tearing down the straw man of an Israelite conquest in the late thirteenth century. He is, in effect, answering questions that few people are asking.

George Kelm argues on the basis of textual analysis and archaeology that the exodus actually occurred in several stages.[42] Although possible, his perspective requires a loose hermeneutical approach.

The Merenptah Stele provides a strong synchronism from the Late Bronze era (fig. 5.2). This inscribed stone slab came to light in Pharaoh Merenptah's mortuary temple in Thebes in 1896. Merenptah, the heir of Ramesses II, announced the extermination of the Israelites:

> Israel is wasted;
> its seed is not.

Egyptian rulers often employed hyperbole (exaggeration) in their inscriptions. This royal propaganda dates to the first few years of Merenptah's reign, around 1209 BC. Aside from Douglas Petrovich's new re-

Fig. 5.2 Merenptah Stele.

search, the stele constitutes the earliest mention of the nation of Israel in the archaeological record, and it indicates that Israel had already prevailed as an established nation by that time. This would not be possible if Israel had just entered the land a few decades before the time of the stele's creation. Time will likely reveal other inscriptions that will document an even earlier presence of Israel in the land of the Bible.

The Route of the Exodus

After centuries of bondage in Egypt, the Israelites finally escaped their oppressors. They journeyed through the sea to Mount Sinai, and eventually to Shittim on the plains of Moab.

The Sea Crossing and Mount Sinai

To date, archaeology has not resolved the issue concerning the locations of the sea crossing or Mount Sinai. Many researchers place Mount Sinai at Jebel Musa, the traditional location in the southern Sinai Peninsula. There has been much written on the Hebrew words *yam sûp*, "the Red Sea" or "the Sea of Reeds." The weight of evidence supports the latter reading, but for now, this remains an ongoing debate that hopefully will be clarified by linguists or epigraphists.[43] Alternatively, the Israelites traveled straight to the Gulf of Aqaba and crossed there. Advocates of this view usually place Mount Sinai at Jebel al-Lawz or at the volcanic Mount Bedr. This option may be supported by the apostle Paul who refers to Mount Sinai as being in Arabia (Gal 4:24–25). However, uncertainty exists regarding the ancient borders of Arabia. Still other scholars posit that Mount Sinai is Har Karkom. For me, a location in the Sinai Peninsula seems most likely.

The Journey to Shittim

The Israelites spent forty years in the Sinai region, near Kadesh Barnea.[44] Their first attempt to enter the promised land followed a straight shot through the Negev. However, they were turned back at Hormah, a site often identified with Tel Masos, near Beersheba.

From there, the Israelites moved eastward to the territory of Edom, but the paranoid Edomite king prohibited their passage. Many interpreters argue that Edom did not develop into a kingdom until the seventh century BC. However, various evidences refute this assertion, such as the topographical lists in Egypt from the time of Thutmose III (fifteenth century BC) to the time of Ramesses II (thirteenth century BC), as well as the work by Thomas Levy at the copper production site of Khirbet en-Nahas.[45]

The Israelites then proceeded to Mount Hor, likely the site of Rekem (later Petra), where Aaron died and was buried. Next they headed back to Arad (Tel ʿArad or Tel Malḥata) in the Negev, where they experienced a military victory. They then traveled eastward, swinging around the territory of Edom before turning north toward Moab. They arrived at Mount Pisgah on the edge of the eastern *kikār* where they battled Sihon and the Amorites, winning victories at Heshbon, Jahaz, and Dibon (modern Dhiban)

(Num 21:10–20). Next, they moved north and defeated Og, the king of Bashan (vv. 33–35).

After these battles, Israel camped on the plains of Moab. The Moabite king, Balak, hired the enigmatic prophet Balaam to curse the Israelites. Numbers 22 records the Balaam account, as does a plaster inscription excavated in 1967 at Tell Deir ʿAlla in Jordan. The thirty-four line inscription begins with these words:

> The misfortunes of the book of Balaam, son of Beor. He was a divine seer.

The inscription dates to the ninth century BC. It retells a story that had circulated the region for hundreds of years and was embedded in the belief system of the indigenous population.

Following the Balaam incident, the Israelites moved south and waged war against the land of Midian, where Moses had spent forty years in exile, and where he had seen the Messenger of Yahweh. Here the Israelites routed five kings. Finally, they settled at Shittim, the last place they camped before they began the conquest of the Cis-Jordan.

The Identification of Shittim

Shittim, also called Abel-Shittim, is only a few miles east of Jericho, on the opposite side the Jordan River. Cartographers generally identify Shittim as Tell el-Ḥammam (cf. Zondervan's *Archaeological Study Bible*). However, some scholars suggest nearby sites such as Tell Kefrein and Tell Nimrin.

Three Bible verses shed light on the location of Shittim: Joshua 2:1 ("Joshua son of Nun sent two spies from Shittim"), Joshua 3:1 ("Joshua and all the Israelites set out from Shittim"), and Numbers 25:1 ("While Israel was staying in Shittim, the men began to indulge in sexual immorality with Moabite women"). With these verses in mind and a Bible handbook or dictionary, an alert reader can sleuth out at least four clues concerning the site's location:

1. Shittim sat across from Jericho.
2. Shittim in Hebrew means "the acacias" and Abel-Shittim means "the meadow of the acacias" or "the brook by the

acacias."

3. The texts never mention architectural features such as walls or gates, people or city officials, nor is there any reference to a battle to oust any inhabitants from Shittim.

4. A good water source existed at the site.

How does Tell el-Ḥammam filter through this criterial screen?

1. Tell el-Ḥammam sits across from Jericho. However, so does almost everything else in the eastern kikār. The crescent shaped Transjordanian mountains on the east and the Jordan River on the west form the diminutive region. The western half of the kikār measures about the same size. The Cisjordanian mountains on the west and the Jordan River on the east provide the regional boundaries. Jericho sits on the edge of the western kikār, so in effect, everything is more or less directly across from it.

2. Based on the meaning of the name Shittim, Acacia groves likely flourished in this area in the Late Bronze Age; however, they have long since disappeared, and banana groves, citrus, and cabbage fields have mostly replaced them. Acacia trees can grow in the harshest of climates, and a few can still be found in the area. To date, no analysis has been performed that would reveal the types of trees around the site during the Late Bronze Age timeframe, or the types of wood used for construction.

3. The Bible does not refer to Shittim as a city. There is no record that Joshua and the Israelites battled (or greeted) anyone once they reached the eastern kikār. The first decade of excavation at Tell el-Ḥammam failed to reveal evidence of occupation in the Late Bronze Age. However, in 2015 a small amount of Late Bronze Age remains appeared.

4. Tell el-Ḥammam has two water sources. First, several perennial springs (hot and cold) grace the site, and provide the basis for its modern name. Tell el-Ḥammam in Arabic means "hill of the hot bath." A second water source is the Wadi Kefrein. When it rained on occasion, the wadi would

channel water right by the site. Based on this alone, it is likely that at least some of the Israelites encamped at Tell el-Ḥammam. A reliable water source would not have been overlooked or bypassed.

The biggest problem with Tell el-Ḥammam as Shittim has to do with numbers. Estimates of the size of the Israelite people range from thirty thousand to several million. Tell el-Ḥammam, the largest site on the eastern *kikār*, could have handled a maximum of about fifteen thousand people on and around the site. In other words, Tell el-Ḥammam could not have possibly accommodated the Israelites, even at the lowest estimate of their population. Today, the eastern *kikār* is home to about sixty-five thousand inhabitants and is pretty full. The area could handle more, perhaps double that number, but it would at some point result in unrealistic population densities. It would have required almost the entire eastern *kikār* to fit the Israelites; therefore, Shittim is likely a description of the region, perhaps with Tell el-Ḥammam as the epicenter.

The Conquest of Canaan

Assuming a date of 1446 BC for the exodus, followed by forty years of wandering, the conquest and settlement of Canaan began around 1406 BC. Scholars posit alternative models for the conquest, but all of them require a minimizing of the biblical text. In the 1920s, Albrecht Alt advanced the possibility of a peaceful infiltration into the land. In the late 1960s and early 1970s, George Mendenhall and Norman Gottwald developed the theory of a peasant uprising.

The Dismay of the Canaanites

The presence of the encroaching Israelites caused dismay among the inhabitants of Canaan, according to the Amarna letters. The Amarna letters constitute an archive of 382 tablets from Tell el-Amarna (Akhetaten) in Egypt (fig. 5.3). A woman discovered the letters in 1887 while digging for fertilizer for her garden. According to the letters, Canaanite vassals corresponded with the Egyptian pharaohs of the mid-fourteenth century BC. There was also correspondence with the Hittite and Mitanni rulers in Anatolia. The letters reveal serious weaknesses among the city-states of the Levant, just after the time of the biblical conquest. Abdi-Heba, the king of Jerusalem, begged the pharaoh to send him a few archers to protect the city from invaders known as the

Figure 5.3. Amarna tablet

Habiru (EA 286–287). The pharaoh was probably Akhenaten (Amenhotep IV), the heretical and monotheistic pharaoh. Labayu, the king of Shechem, admits a confederacy of his own son with these invaders (EA 252–254).

The pharaoh never responded to the appeals of his vassals, thus indicating an unwillingness or inability to protect them. His silence illustrates the weakened state of Egypt after the biblical plagues and the exodus of the Israelites. A strong case can be made that the term *Hebrew* relates to Habiru, although it may encompass groups other than just the Israelites. For example, the Egyptian texts refer to a group of nomadic encroachers in the Transjordan region of Edom and Moab known as the Shasu. In a more general sense, the Shasu may also refer to the Habiru.[46]

The Defeat of Jericho

The conquest of western Canaan began at Jericho. Four teams have excavated Jericho, and each team has arrived at somewhat different conclusions from the data.[47] Jericho was first excavated from 1907 to 1909 by Germans Ernst Sellin and Carl Watzinger. Sellin and Watzinger found that most of the Bronze Age wall had collapsed. However, a portion of the lower city wall remained standing. This stretch of the wall had houses attached to it and was located between the inner and outer walls. The discovery supports the statements about Rahab's house in Joshua 2:18–19 and 6:17–23.

John Garstang excavated prolifically from Egypt to Turkey, but he remains best known for his work at Jericho from 1930 to 1936. He dated the destruction of City IV to approximately 1400 BC, which matches the biblical date. As part of his meticulous and innovative field methodology, Garstang photographed material in situ prior to excavation.

From 1952 to 1958, Kathleen Kenyon conducted the most extensive excavations at Jericho. Kenyon employed excellent methodology that surpassed that of her predecessors. She dated the massive destruction of the site (City IV) to the end of the Middle Bronze Age. However, several scarabs of the Eighteenth Egyptian Dynasty date City IV to the fifteenth century BC. Bryant Wood reexamined and reinterpreted much of Kenyon's data and assigned it a Late Bronze Age date, thus demonstrating perfect harmony with Garstang's conclusions and the Joshua narrative (cf. fig. 5.4).

Figure 5.4. Bichrome ware from Jericho

For the past decade, Sapienza University of Rome and the Palestinian Authority have excavated at Jericho. Little has been published, but the lead excavator, professor Lorenzo Nigro, favors Kenyon's paradigm.

The Defeat of Ai and the Covenant Ceremony

After conquering Jericho, the Israelites turned their attention to the small fortress of Ai. Initially, the location of Ai proved problematic for archaeologists because the proposed site—et-Tell, according to Albright—was much larger than the sites of Gibeon and Jericho. His identification contradicted the biblical account. Close examination revealed that a large Early Bronze to Intermediate Bronze Age city once thrived at et-Tell. Moreover, the site sat unoccupied in the Late Bronze Age. The resolution of the contradiction lay in Albright's partial misidentification of the site. While the Ai of the Intermediate Bronze Age likely existed at et-Tell, it clearly was not the Ai of the Late Bronze Age.

Nineteenth century AD scholars Edward Robinson and Ernst Sellin reported a local tradition that Ai was actually located at modern Khirbet el-Maqatir. From 1995 to 2016, the Associates for Biblical Research excavated Khirbet el-Maqatir, a site that meets all the geographical and chronological parameters for Joshua's Ai. Bryant Wood led this excavation through 2013, and I directed the final three seasons of the dig through 2016. This effort proved beyond a reasonable doubt that the remains of Ai of Joshua 7–8 lie at Khirbet el-Maqatir.[48]

Subsequent to the demise of Ai, Joshua built an altar on Mount Ebal, near Mount Gerizim in Samaria (Josh 8:30). The instructions regarding the altar were given by Moses to Joshua in Deuteronomy 27:4: "when you have crossed over the Jordan you shall set up these stones, about which I am commanding you today, on Mount Ebal, and you shall cover them with plaster." It was at this place that Joshua initially apportioned the land to the various tribes. He later completed this process at Shiloh (Josh 18). Israeli archaeologist Adam Zertal excavated and restored an altar on Mount Ebal.[49] As I see it, the altar closely resembled the altar of the temple although 300 years earlier.

The Defeat of Hazor

Hazor, the largest site conquered by Joshua and the Israelites, represented the ultimate prize. Joshua 11:10 describes Hazor as chief among the Canaanite kingdoms. The Amarna letters reinforce the city's prominence. Yigael Yadin first excavated Hazor (Tell el-Qedah). Later, his protégé, Amnon Ben Tor, led long-term excavations at the massive site. Eight fragments of cuneiform tablets have been found so far, and there seems little doubt that an archive awaits discovery at the site. Ben Tor, now in his eighties, remains steadfast in his efforts. Both Yadin and Ben Tor found abundant evidence of burning and destruction at Hazor at the time of the conquest—a synchronism with Joshua 11:11. The metropolis, with its large wall and impressive defensive fortifications, apparently underwent rebuilding rather quickly, only to be destroyed again, probably by Deborah and Barak (Judg 4–5). Solomon later fortified Hazor, likely an administrative center (1 Kgs 9:15). Excavations at Hazor and Khirbet el-Maqatir both yield evidence of the iconoclastic decapitation of figurines or idols.[50]

The Settlement of the Land

Interestingly, the biblical books of Joshua and Judges emphasize different aspects of the conquest and settlement. Joshua portrays the conquest as a total victory that was achieved with lightning fast speed. The book of Judges, on the other hand, tells of a long and protracted process that resulted in only partial victory (Judg 1:19–26). The archaeological record confirms the incompleteness of the conquest. In fact, the Bible reveals that many of the Canaanite tribes remained in the land after the initial conquest. The Israelites spared the Shechemites, most likely because of their connection to the patriarchs, and the Gibeonites became servants of the Israelites. An Amalakite killed King Saul, and one of David's champions, Uriah, was a Hethite. In addition, the Philistines entered Canaan in the early twelfth century BC and became a separate and potent political force.

The archaeology on the east side of the Jordan lags far behind that of the west side. Efforts in the east are just beginning to illumine the proto-Israelite settlements of Reuben, Gad, and the half-tribe of Manasseh. The Madaba Plains Project excavated and restored a four-room house at Tell el-'Umayri in the tribal allotment of Gad. (For the significance of a four-room house, see

Figure 5.5. Temple at Shechem

chapter 6.) Current excavations at Tell el-Ḥammam and Khirbet el-Medeineh—both in the region of ancient Moab and modern Jordan—as well as excavations at Tell Jalul portend clarity to this emerging picture.

In the Cisjordan, Yahweh, the God of the Israelites, continued to live in the tabernacle (tent) at Shiloh, while the polytheistic Canaanites had a plethora of temples at which they worshipped their deities. Temples existed at Megiddo, Lachish, Beit Shean, Shechem, and Hazor. The temple at Shechem can likely be identified with the temple of el-Berith mentioned in Judges 9:46 (fig. 5.5). The temple contained a large standing stone, which appears to have been broken in half in antiquity. The break is certainly not modern. The temple at Hazor contained multiple standing stones and other religious paraphernalia, such as statues and cult stands.

Figure 5.6. Possible locations of the tabernacle at Shiloh

At some point, the Shiloh tabernacle may have transitioned into a more permanent temple. The new dig at Shiloh, under my direction, will address this matter among other research goals. Of particular interest to the reader will be the location of the ancient Israelite cultic shrine. Figure 5.6 displays three possible locations of the tabernacle at Shiloh: (1) north of the tell, as proposed by Wilson and Kaufman; (2) the summit of the tell (Kjaer and Finkelstein), and (3) south of the tell (Avi-Yonah and Garfinkel). I propose that the tabernacle first rested on the summit, then relocated to the northern or southern location when it became a permanent building in Iron Age I.[51]

The End of the Late Bronze Age

The Late Bronze Age civilization in the Levant came to an abrupt and violent end, much like the Middle Bronze Age that preceded it. Several factors caused the cultural collapse. First, the pressure from the upstart Habiru created tremendous problems for the Canaanite city-states, especially when pharaoh did not respond to their appeals for help, per the Amarna letters. Second, the invasion of the Philistines and other Sea Peoples into the coastal plain made it even more difficult for the native population to access the seaports and the *Via Maris*, both of which were essential for trade.

Third, the entire Mediterranean basin, especially Mycenae and Crete, experienced upheaval due to natural disasters and other factors. The upheavals further disrupted the economy of Palestine. And fourth, the climate of the Late Bronze Age saw less precipitation than the preceding eras. In the end, the old Canaanite system finally collapsed under its own weight and ultimately underwent reconstruction on a new social blueprint—that of the emerging Israelites.

Further Study and Discussion

What are the evidences of cultural decline in the Late Bronze Age?

How can the exodus and conquest be dated using internal biblical chronology?

What insights can be gained from the Amarna tablets?

Who were the Habiru?

The unexamined life is not worth living.

❖ Socrates

Chapter 6

The Iron Age

Shortly after 1200 BC, a new culture began to emerge in the Levant. The Late Bronze Age city-states had finally collapsed due to a number of factors: pressure from the Habiru, invasion of the Sea Peoples, and major upheaval in the eastern Mediterranean basin.

The Iron Age extended from 1177 BC to 587 BC. Prior to this period, most of the heavily wooded areas of the central hill country remained unsettled. However, archaeologists have identified hundreds of new villages in the hill country from this era. The thickest concentration of these new villages lies between Shechem and Hebron, but the villages also reached to the Shephelah and Golan regions. In the tribal allotment of Benjamin alone, new villages appear at numerous sites: Tell el-Ful, Khirbet el-Maqatir, Khirbet el-Burj, Hizma, el-Jib (Gibeon), Jaba, Khirbet ed-Dawwara, Mukhmas, Khirbet Tell el-Askar, Khirbet Nisya, et-Tell, Khirbet Radanna, Rammun, Ras et-Tahune, and Beitin. These villages clearly represent the spread of a new monotheistic culture—the Israelite culture.

During Iron Age I (1177–950 BC), Israel transitioned from a loose confederation of tribes to a united monarchy that had the ability to levy taxes and complete monumental construction projects. Iron Age I potters produced inferior pottery. Iron Age II (950–587 BC), however, witnessed the improvement of the potter's fast wheel. The introduction of the fast wheel resulted in the proliferation of pottery and pottery types. As mentioned, each period has its unique ceramic forms. For example, after the fall of the Northern Kingdom of Israel to Assyria, a new type of pottery, Assyrian palace ware, appears in the archaeological record.

Cultural Characteristics of the Early Israelites

Figure 6.1. Four-room Israelite house at Hazor

Five cultural characteristics distinguish the early Israelite settlements from the non-Israelite settlements. These distinctives signal Israelite habitation in the highlands of Israel.

Four-Room Houses

The name *four-room house* is actually misleading. Only the first floor had four rooms, and none of the second floors have survived. Stone construction characterized the first floors, while mud-brick normally constituted the primary construction material for the second floor. If the second stories used stone construction, we would expect some examples to have survived.

The first floor served utilitarian purposes, such as storage, cooking, and shelter for livestock. The second floor provided living and sleeping space for the family. Roofs functioned as multipurpose space.[52] Basic pillared-courtyard construction first appeared near the end of Late Bronze Age. It became more common in Iron Age I and ubiquitous in Iron Age II, west of the

Jordan, at sites such as Beersheba, Hazor, Khirbet Radanna, Giloh, and ʿIzbet Ṣarṭah. These indicative dwellings have also been found east of the Jordan at Tawilan, Tell el-ʿUmayri (near Amman), and Khirbet en-Nahas (on the plateau near the southern end of the Dead Sea).

The four-room house reflects the biblical concept of *mišpāḥâ*, the father's house or the extended family dwelling (cf. Judges and Samuel). The four-room house may mirror the special arrangements of the tents in which the Israelites lived for forty years.[53] While scholars remain divided on whether early houses reflected special arrangements carried over from nomadic living, the theory merits consideration. If the hypothesis proves true, the

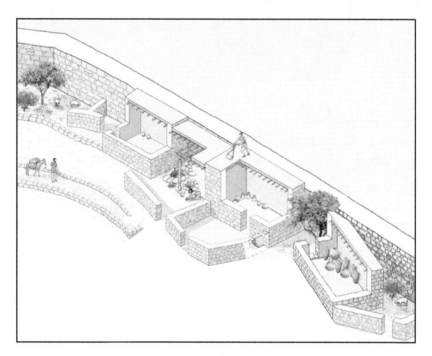

Figure 6.2. Israelite houses at Khirbet el-Maqatir, Iron Age I

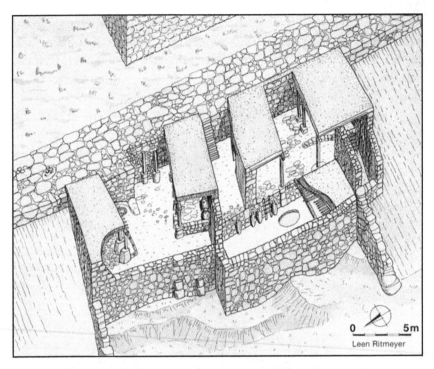

Figure 6.3. Israelite houses or storerooms at Shiloh, Iron Age I

layout of the four-room house, which appears similar to that of the tabernacle and later the temple, may reflect an anthropological progression from tent dwelling nomads to a stable and settled people. Yahweh, the god of the Israelites, moved from a tent (tabernacle) to a building (temple) with the same layout. The Israelites possibly built their houses on the same basic floor plan so that each family's home was seen as a temple to Yahweh. Figure 6.1 shows the standard floor plan. Two rooms flank the central courtyard, and a broad room spans the back of the residence. Recreated four-room houses are on display at Tell el-'Umayri, the Harvard Semitic Museum at Cambridge, and the Israel Museum in Jerusalem.

Early in Iron Age I, the residents at Khirbet el-Maqatir built the most primitive Israelite dwellings (fig. 6.2). A generation later, more advanced pillared-courtyard dwellings were built at Shiloh, in Area C (fig. 6.3). With the passage of another generation, the standard four-room house represented the new status quo in home construction.

Collared-Rim Jars

The characteristic feature of collared-rim storage jars is a raised collar on the shoulder where the neck attaches to the body of the vessel (fig. 6.4). In the highlands, these jars are found in high concentrations at sites identified as Israelite, and in low concentrations at sites not identified with the Israelites. They appear in the middle of the Late Bronze Age and pass from the archaeological record around 900 BC.

Figure 6.4. Collared-rim jar (pithos) from Khirbet el-Maqatir

Red-slipped Burnished Pottery

Like the collared-rim jar, red-slipped burnished pottery appears frequently at sites normally identified with the Israelites and almost never at non-Israelite sites. Before the vessel is fired in a kiln, the potter applies a slip, a mixture of water and reddish clay.[54] This process came into vogue in the late eleventh century BC, during the reign of King Saul. It remained popular in both the north and south, even after the division of the kingdom around 920 BC.

Agricultural Terraces

The deforestation of the central hill country created an immediate threat of losing the fertile topsoil due to erosion from wind and rain. As a result, the Israelites developed a system of terracing that, in effect, created a series of step-like platforms (fig. 1.3). As the Israelites removed the rocks from the soil (a necessity for farming), they used them to build the retaining walls of the terraces. Eventually, this new farming technology spread around the world. Shimon Gibson wrote his doctoral dissertation on terraces, and he is the leading expert in Israel on the topic.

Absence of Pig Bones

Only a small percentage of bones found at traditional Israelite sites belong to pigs. A much higher percentage of pig bones exist at non-Israelite sites. Most archaeologists attribute this discrepancy to the prohibition in the Torah against consumption of pork (Deut 14:8).

An ethnic indicator rarely occurs without the presence of other ethnic indicators. Therefore, an absence of pig bones at a site often coincides with the presence of collared-rim jars and four-room houses. Shiloh provides a good example of this. West of the tell in Area C, both Kjaer and Finkelstein excavated pillared courtyard-buildings that were constructed against the outside of the Bronze Age wall. These structures yielded two-dozen collared-rim jars, which were the typical Iron Age I pithos type in the Israel highlands. Finkelstein suggests, and I agree, that the Middle Bronze Age storerooms in Areas F–H served a central shrine.55 The same is likely true of the Iron Age pillared courtyard-buildings in Area C. In Area D, northwest of the tell, Finkelstein uncovered a massive bone deposit and abundant Late Bronze Age ceramics, including cultic vessels. The array of faunal remains corresponded to the animals of the biblical sacrificial system—sheep, goats, and a smaller amount of cattle. At Shiloh, pig bones comprised (a) 3.5 percent of the Middle Bronze II bones, (b) less than 2 percent of the Late Bronze Age assemblage, and (c) less than 1 percent in Iron Age I.[56] The percentage of pig bones reduced by more than half when the site moved from Amorite control to Israelite control.

The Late Bronze Age bone deposit likely indicates cultic activity on the summit.

Figure 6.5. Archaeologists Scott Stripling (*left*) and Eli Shukron (*right*)

The United Kingdom

In the middle of Iron Age I (ca. 1040 BC), the nation of Israel transitioned from a confederacy of tribes ruled by regional judges to a centralized monarchy. Saul became Israel's first king, and he reigned from about 1040 BC to 1000 BC. David succeeded him and centralized the administration of the kingdom in the fortress of Zion that he had captured from the Jebusites. The city of David, just over ten acres, has been probed and excavated by a number of archaeologists and explorers, including Charles Warren, Kathleen Kenyon, Eilat Mazar, Ronny Reich, and Eli Shukron (fig. 6.5). With the establishment of a centralized administration, the Israelites began to leave their mark on the archaeological record through official records and seals as well as monumental building projects.[57]

Charles Warren discovered a vertical water shaft, now called Warren's Shaft. The shaft allowed access to the Gihon Spring from inside "the fortress of Zion" (Hebrew: *məṣudat ṣiyôn*). Joab and David's other mighty men possibly used a shaft in order to enter the city and oust the Jebusites (cf. 1 Chr 11:6).

Prior to 1993, no extrabiblical materials attested to King David. That all changed with the discovery of the Tel Dan Stele, also known as the house of David inscription (fig. 6.6).[58] This Aramaic inscription, dating to the mid-ninth century BC, refers to the "house of David" and the "kingdom of Israel." The discovery illustrates Kenneth Kitchen's maxim: "Absence of evidence is not evidence of absence." Kitchen has also pointed out Pharaoh Shoshenq's reference to the "heights of David" on a monumental inscription in Egypt. Scholars such as André Lemaire believe that a mention of the "house of David" also appears on the ninth-century BC Moabite Stone. Many more biblical characters and events will, no doubt, be substantiated in the years ahead.

Eilat Mazar's excavation of the Large Stone Structure likely revealed David's actual palace, just above the well-known Stepped Stone Structure or *milô*. All but the most skeptical of scholars accept this identification. Minimalists demonize Mazar for daring to connect archaeological findings with the biblical text.

The first truly monumental architecture in Israel was built by David's son, Solomon, who ruled from about 970 BC to 930 BC. Solomon's fame ties, in large part, to the great temple he constructed. Unfortunately, no verifiable remnants of this temple survived the Babylonian razing in 587 BC, although Peretz Reuven argues convincingly that the beams from the al-Aqsa Mosque may have originally supported the Jewish temples. An inscribed ivory pomegranate, once thought to function as the head of a priestly scepter from Solomon's temple, now bears the ignominy of being a forgery. Later, rival temples to Yahweh would be built on Mount Gerizim in Samaria, on the island of Elephantine in Egypt, and at Arad in the Negev.[59] Solomon had foreign help in building his temple. As David Graves writes,

Figure 6.6. House of David inscription

A mutual contract was agreed upon between Solomon and King Hiram, and Hiram supplied lumber and craftsmen in return for food for the royal household (1 Kgs 5). Hiram was "a worker in bronze. And he was full of wisdom, understanding, and skill for making any work in bronze" (1 Kgs 7:14). He made all the bronze furnishings for the temple including two pillars named Jachin and Boaz (1 Kgs 7:15–22, 41–42; 2 Chr 3:15–17; 2 Kgs 25:16–17; Jer 52:17, 20–23) and the bronze sea (equivalent to the laver in the temple but much larger). There was so much bronze used, Solomon left it all unweighed (1 Kgs 7:40–47). The biblical record is accompanied by Phoenician records written by Sanchuniathan, an 8th century BC priest. He wrote of how Hiram would provide the ruler of Judah with building supplies in return for seaport facilities. Sanchuniathan states that the lumber was transported by 8,000 camels. Also, 1 Kings 9:27 mentions "seamen who were familiar with the sea," and the Phoenician priest gives the names of these mariners as Kedarus, Jaminus and Kotilus.... The closet parallel to the Jerusalem temple is the 9th cent. temple at Tell Ta'yinnat in northern Syria uncovered in 1936. The interesting features of this structure are the rectangular shape and its division into three sections. The Jerusalem temple similarly contained an entrance hall, main hall, and the holy of holies. Both structures had pillars although the pillars of the Ta'yinnat temple were built under the roof of the Syrian sanctuary which was 2/3 smaller than Solomon's temple.[60]

Evidence of Solomon's architectural prowess appears throughout Israel. Most notable are the six-chambered gates at Hazor, Gezer, and Megiddo (fig. 6.7). First Kings 9:15 mentions these three cities as having been fortified by Solomon. The existence of almost identical gate complexes at these three important sites is another strong convergence of the archaeological data and the biblical text. Each of the gate complexes joined a casemate wall system that encircled the city. Casemate walls consist of two parallel walls supported by perpendicular braces at periodic intervals. In addition to protection, the casemate walls provided storage and domestic dwellings. Six-chambered gates have also been identified at Tel Lachish (thirty miles southwest of Jerusalem) and Khirbet el-Medeineh (north of the Wadi Mujib in modern Jordan).

Figure 6.7. Solomonic gate at Hazor

The Gezer Calendar dates to late in the united kingdom and serves as one of the earliest examples of widespread literacy in Israel. The calendar documents the seasons for various agricultural functions. Not all scholars agree that the script is written in Hebrew.

The Divided Kingdom

Many Iron Age inscriptions verify the accuracy of the biblical text. The British Museum in London and the Louvre in Paris house many of these inscriptions.

Two synchronisms pertain to Tiglath-pileser III, the king of Assyria from about 745 BC to 727 BC. The Bible refers to this monarch nine times. The Iran Stele and the Annals of Tiglath-pileser III mention King Menahem of Israel paying tribute to him. The annals from Tiglath-pileser III's palace in Calah, Iraq, likewise twice mention King Pekah of Israel. A royal seal of Israel from the same period depicts Pekah, another king of Israel with the same name.

A century before Tiglath-pileser III, another Assyrian despot, Shalmaneser III, had a large black obelisk created to record and portray the foreign kings who served as his vassals (fig. 6.8). Among the foreign kings is Jehu, King of Israel.[61] The inscription states,

Figure 6.8. Black Obelisk of Shalmaneser III

I received the tribute of Jehu of the house of Omri.

The obelisk affirms the existence of Jehu and reveals his physical likeness, but the Bible does not mention the tribute. Importantly, the artifact reminds us that the Bible does not present fictional characters.

The Kurkh Stele, also known as the Monolith of Shalmaneser III, mentions the Assyrian despot's dealings with the infamous king Ahab of Israel and Ben Hadad of Damascus. First Kings 22 also records their conflict.

The Northern Kingdom of Israel fell to Sargon II and the Assyrians in 722 BC. Sargon's annals record the following:

I besieged and conquered Samaria, and carried away 22,290 inhabitants.

Figure 6.9. Lachish relief showing the Assyrian siege

As a result, a flood of refugees poured into Judah during the coregency of Ahaz and his son Hezekiah.[62] Upon Ahaz's death in 715 BC, Hezekiah became the sole monarch over Judah. Hezekiah promptly refurbished the Jerusalem temple and extended the city wall to take in the northern refugees, thus expanding Jerusalem to four times its previous size. Hezekiah, a loyal vassal of Sargon II until the Assyrian monarch's death in 705 BC, joined with other Assyrian vassals in an attempt to gain independence. The new Assyrian monarch, Sennacherib, responded by invading Judah in 701 BC. In 1850, a series of twelve continuous reliefs came to light in Sennacherib's palace in Nineveh. The huge reliefs depict the siege and fall of Lachish, an important city that protected the ascent to Jerusalem from the southwest (fig. 6.9).

In preparation for a time of siege, Hezekiah commissioned workers to cut a tunnel through the limestone core of Mount Zion in order to redirect the flow of the Gihon Spring to an area inside the city wall, thus creating the pool of Siloam (2 Chr 32:1–5). Two teams worked from opposite ends, and where they met, Hezekiah commissioned an inscription to commemorate the achievement. A boy bathing in the tunnel in 1880 discovered the inscription. The Siloam Inscription is on display at the Istanbul Archaeological Museum. It explains,

> The tunneling was completed ... while the hewers yielded the axe, each man toward the other, axe against axe, the water flowed from the spring to the pool, a distance of twelve hundred cubits.

According to the Bible, God smote the Assyrian army, resulting in 185,000 deaths. Sennacherib's annals confirm the battle, but they record a very different perspective:

> I left Hezekiah caged like a bird in Jerusalem.

Two separate prisms confirm Hezekiah's rebellion and Sargon's ultimate retreat.

Many other important inscriptions represent Iron Age II. The ostraca, stelae, and bullae corroborate biblical events and persons.

Jehoash Inscription

The Tell al-Rimah Stele, discovered in Iraq in 1967, mentions Jehoash, who reigned from about 798 BC to 782 BC. The stele records the Levantine campaign by the Assyrian king Adadnirani in 796 BC. Among those reported to have paid tribute was "Joash the Samarian." Joash and Jehoash are variant spellings of the same name.

Samaria Ostraca

Sixty-three ostraca were unearthed in 1910 at Sebaste
(Samaria). Most of the ostraca
contain receipts for oil and
wine. More importantly, the
ostraca use many of the clan
names from the tribe of
Manasseh, which inherited the
territory of Samaria (Josh
17:1–4; fig. 6.10).

Figure 6.10. One of the Samaria
ostraca

Moabite Stone

In 1868, near Dhiban, Jordan, local bedouin discovered an
inscribed basalt slab, known as the Moabite Stone or the Mesha
Stele. The inscription refers to Yahweh, the God of the Israelites,
and Chemosh, the Moabite deity representing the sun. The
inscription proclaims,

> I am Mesha, son of Chemos ... King of Moab, the
> Dibonite.... My father ruled over Moab thirty years,
> and I ruled after my father. And I made this high
> place to Chemosh because of the deliverance of
> Mesha, because he saved me from all the kings and
> caused me to see my desire upon all who hated me.
> Omri, king of Israel, oppressed Moab many days
> because Chemosh was angry with his land. And his
> son succeeded him, and he also said I will oppress
> Moab. In my days he spoke according to his word,
> but I saw my desire upon him and upon his house,
> and Israel perished with an everlasting loss. Now
> Omri had possessed all the land of Medeba and
> dwelt in it in his days and half the days of his son
> ... but Chemosh restored it in my day.

The inscription and 2 Kings 3 agree that Mesha revolted against the control of Israel's king Joram (Jehoram). The stele also mentions that the tribe of Gad settled the region of Moab in the ninth century BC, thus confirming Numbers 32:34.

Ahaz Bulla

In Iron Age II, the divided kingdom, scribes would seal important documents with a lump of clay bearing their signet impression. The impressed clay is called a bulla (plural: bullae). When fire destroyed the ancient document, it hardened and preserved the impressed clay. The Ahaz Bulla or Jotham Bulla dates to the mid-eighth century BC. It reads as follows:

> Belonging to Ahaz (son of) Jotham, king of Judah.

Second Kings 16:1 mentions both kings: "Ahaz the son of Jotham." The bulla appears to have been impressed by the personal seal of Ahaz.

Shishak Relief

Pharaoh Sheshonk (Shoshenq), probably referred to in the Bible as Shishak, ruled Egypt from 945 BC to 924 BC. A relief on his temple at Karnak portrays his Levantine expedition, known from 1 Kings 14 and 2 Chronicles 12. A fragment of Shishak's victory stele, celebrating the success of his campaign, was unearthed at Tel Megiddo in 1926. Once again, the Bible describes real people, places, and events.

Bullae from Jeremiah's Time

Bullae representing several names mentioned in Jeremiah emerged from the 587 BC destruction debris in the city of David. Seven bullae, found in close proximity to the palace, likely confirm the historicity of Jeremiah's account:

Elishama (cf. 36:12)
Gamariah (cf. 36:10–27)
Gedaliah, son of Immer (cf. 20:1)

Gedaliah, son of Pashur (cf. 38:1)
Jaazaniah (cf. 40:8)
Jucal (cf. 37:3; 38:1)
Ishmael (cf. 40:8)

Other names in the book of Jeremiah appear on seals, ostraca, and inscriptions. Importantly, forgers produced two bullae ascribed to Baruch, Jeremiah's scribe. Although early reports indicated the authenticity of the two bullae, eventually scholars recognized them as forgeries. Forged antiquities present a serious challenge to the academic community because they require someone with a high level of expertise to produce them.

The Philistines

Around 1177 BC, the Philistines and other Sea Peoples gained control of the coastal plain. The Philistines interacted extensively with the Israelites, but other tribes of Sea Peoples existed as well: Tjekker, Danuna, Sherden (Sherdani), Tursha, Ekwesh, Sheklesh, and Lukka. The ten references to the Philistines in Genesis and Exodus may be anachronistic, but it is more likely that groups of Sea Peoples from Mycenae, Crete, and the Aegean basin had already established colonies centuries before the main migration in the twelfth century.[63] They were technologically more advanced than the other inhabitants of the Levant. In the mortuary temple of Ramesses III at Medinet Habu in Egypt, a huge relief tells the story of the pharaoh's victory over the Sea People. Though strong, they failed to capture Egypt.

The cities of the core Philistine pentapolis include Ekron, Ashkelon, Ashdod, Gaza, and Gath. These cities have all been excavated, at least partially. As stated, Philistine technology surpassed that of the native Canaanites and the upstart Israelites. Judges 13:19–20 indicates that the Philistines maintained a monopoly on iron technology during Iron Age I. Since no evidence exists of iron working among the Israelites until the time of David, it seems likely that David acquired iron technology during his stay among the Philistines at Ziklag (1 Sam 27). Philistine pottery was initially unique and easily recognizable. The Philistines preferred bichrome pottery with black and red paint. Their favorite motifs were concentric circles and a swan with its head turned backward (fig. 6.11). Gradually the Philistine pottery and language assimilated to the surrounding nations. The highest concentration of Philistine pottery has been found in the pentapolis; however, many other sites such as Gezer Beit Shean have also produced impressive amounts.

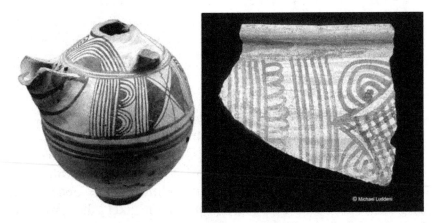

Figure 6.11. *Left*, Philistine jar from Beth-Shemesh; *right*, Philistine pottery with typical concentric circles

In 2006, an inscription dating to around 1000 BC was unearthed at Tell eṣ-Ṣafi (Gath) (fig. 6.12). The inscription may mention the name Goliath from the monumental battle of David and Goliath (1 Sam 17). Trude Dothan and Seymour Gitin excavated for fifteen years at Tel Miqne (Ekron), a large site of more than fifty acres. A huge olive processing industry stands out among the impressive finds. David Ussishkin challenged their claim that Ekron was fortified in Iron Age I, but he failed to convince many of his colleagues.

© David E. Graves

cm

Figure 6.12. Goliath (?) inscription from Gath

While Ashkelon dates to the Early Bronze Age, the most impressive remains come from the Early Roman Era. According to one tradition, Herod the Great was born there, and he later built elaborate public works in honor of his hometown. Very little work has been done at Gaza because of the urban sprawl and violence of the modern city. Excavation depends upon peace in the Gaza strip, so it will likely be many years before the material culture can be fully examined.

Further Study and Discussion

What is the cultural significance of the four-room house?

Why was the discovery of the "house of David" inscription important?

In the context of archaeology, what is a synchronism? Give examples.

How did the Philistines differ from the Canaanites and the Israelites?

The great thing about being married to an archaeologist is that the older I get, the more interesting he finds me.

❖ Agatha Christie

Chapter 7

The Babylonian, Persian, and Hellenistic Ages

An important time in the land of the Bible unfolded between the destruction of the First Temple to the Hellenistic Age. This chapter explores the archaeological remains from these centuries.

Babylonian Evidence

Nebuchadnezzar of Babylon ruled from about 605 BC to 562 BC. He imposed Babylonian hegemony upon the Levant. Dozens of extrabiblical attestations establish the existence of Nebuchadnezzar, and the Bible mentions him more than any other foreign king. Nebuchadnezzar's annals refer to the final three kings of Judah: Jehoiakim, Jehoiachin, and Zedekiah. When Zedekiah rebelled in 589 BC, Nebuchadnezzar responded by destroying the cities of Judah, including Jerusalem. The temple was plundered and burned in August of 587 BC, and many more Jews became captives. The destruction marked the end of the Iron Age, although 587–332 BC is sometimes referred to as Iron Age III.

Second Kings 25:27–30 and Jeremiah 52:31–34 indicate that King Jehoiachin was taken captive to Babylon. Four cuneiform tablets found in a palace at Babylon confirm the presence of Jehoiachin among a group of foreign dignitaries who were under the patronage of the Babylonian despot.

The Lachish ostraca bear witness to the destruction of Judah's cities by Nebuchadnezzar (fig. 7.1). In 1935, excavations yielded twenty-one ostraca from a guard-room near the gate of Lachish. Ostracon 3 reveals that an envoy went to Egypt to request aid, which affirms Jeremiah 37: 7–8.[64] Ostracon 4 refers to the watchman's observation that the signal fires from Azekah had ceased to burn. Azekah, the last Judean city to fall prior to Lachish, guarded Jerusalem from the west.

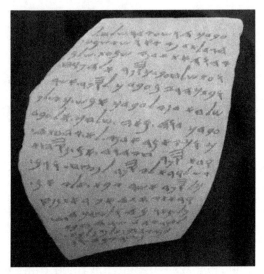

Figure 7.1. Lachish Ostracon 3

Upon the death of Nebuchadnezzar, the throne passed to Nabonidus, who in turn named his son Belshazzar as his co-regent. The first part of his name, Bel, was the chief Babylonian god, also known as Marduk. Like Baal, it could also be used generically of a deity to simply mean lord.

According to Daniel 5, the fall of Babylon to the Persians occurred while Belshazzar and the Babylonian aristocracy partied the night away. The city fell in 539 BC. The Greek historian Herodotus (ca. 480–425 BC) elucidates additional details of that night (*Histories* 1.189–91). According to Herodotus, Cyrus the Persian (Cyrus the Great) redirected the Euphrates River which ran through the center of Babylon, thus allowing his men to enter the city under the water gate. Babylon fell without a battle, according to Herodotus, the Cyrus Cylinder, and the Babylonian Chronicle.

The archaeological record also testifies of Jews in Babylon. In 2016, one hundred cuneiform tablets dating from about 550 BC to 498 BC went on display at the Bible Lands Museum in Jerusalem. The tablets refer to non-native groups living in Babylon at the time. And they use names such as *al yahudu*, meaning, in essence, the "New Jerusalem." The tablets document many aspects of daily life for the exiles in Babylon, including matters of commerce and romance. Other groups such as the Philistines, who were deported at the same time as the Israelites, are mentioned in similar texts by the names of their cities (e.g., Ashkelon and Gaza). Unlike the Israelites, the Philistines did not survive the Babylonian captivity as an identifiable ethnic group, although many Palestinians today believe that they descend from these ancient people.

Persian Evidence

Persian foreign policy reversed that of the Babylonians. Whereas the Babylonians exported native populations from the lands they conquered, the Persians preferred to keep conquered people in their native lands under a governor or satrap. The Cyrus Cylinder, a nine-inch long clay cylinder from 536 BC, confirms their policy. It reads in part:

> I gathered their former inhabitants and returned them.

Figure 7.2. Cyrus Cylinder

This priceless artifact, discovered in 1879, resides in the British Museum in London (fig. 7.2). In 2013, five museums in the United States and one in India displayed the cylinder, which offers the first statement of basic human rights and freedom of religion.

The Cyrus Cylinder evokes Nabonidus. Darius I, sometimes referred to as Darius the Great, continued Cyrus' liberal policy of repatriation. The biblical books of Ezra, Zechariah, and Haggai mention Darius. The trilingual official cylinder seal of Darius resides in the British Museum in London. The three languages on the seal are Persian, Elamite, and Babylonian.

King Xerxes, known in the Bible as Ahasuerus, succeeded Darius as ruler of Persia. His son, King Artaxerxes, allowed the repatriation of Ezra the scribe, and thirteen years later (ca. 445 BC), Nehemiah and other Jews. The book of Nehemiah describes three principal adversaries that Nehemiah faced in his attempt to rebuild Jerusalem's walls: Sanballat, Tobiah, and Geshem (2:9–10). These three men also appear in extrabiblical sources from the fifth to second centuries BC.

A papyrus letter found at Elephantine, Egypt, names Sanballat as the governor of Samaria. It dates to about 407 BC. Other sources indicate that Sanballat's son and grandson bore the same name and also ruled the region of Samaria as a type of dynasty. Tobiah hailed from the Transjordan region. The Tobiah or Tobias family name appears in papyrus from the third century BC and in an inscription at their second-century BC family estate west of Amman at Iraq al-Amir. Geshem hailed from Arabia. An inscription from northern Arabia dating to Nehemiah's time mentions Geshem:

Geshem son of Sahr and Abd, governor of Dedan

The archaeology of the fifth century BC illuminates the biblical text. These three adversaries—Sanballat, Tobiah, and Geshem—were not petty local chieftains, as minimalists and liberals contend; rather, they were powerful and influential regional leaders who posed a serious threat to the rebuilding process of Jerusalem. Indeed, Nehemiah had his hands full, and he needed divine grace and intervention.

Hellenistic Evidence

For almost a century, the Persians battled the Greeks, an emerging world power. After some well-documented losses, such as the battle of Thermopylae in August of 480 BC, the Greeks ultimately prevailed and dominated the world stage until just before the events of the New Testament. The spread of Greek culture is known as hellenization. Isocrates (436–338 BC) explains the Athenian view of Hellenism:

> And so far has our city distanced the rest of mankind in thought and speech that her pupils have become the teachers of the rest of the world; and she has brought it about that the name "Hellenes" suggests no longer a race but an intelligence. And the title "Hellenes" is applied rather to those who share our culture than those who share a common blood. (*Panegyricus* 50)

Hellenization came about through the conquests of the infamous leader, Alexander the Great.

Alexander the Great

In 356 BC, Alexander the Great was born to Phillip II of Macedon. King Phillip hired the renowned Greek philosopher Aristotle to educate his young son who proved to be exceptionally bright and equally ambitious. Alexander ultimately conquered the entire Mediterranean world in twelve years (334–323 BC).

Alexander loved his physical appearance. As a result, many extant sculptures, paintings, and coins bear his image (fig. 7.3). Even the people he conquered seemed enamored by him, as evidenced by the Alexander mosaic excavated in 2015 in the Huquq synagogue. Museums around the world, such as the Istanbul Archaeological Museum, display exceptional life-size busts of this remarkable ruler.

Alexander died at the early age thirty-three (ca. 323 BC). He did not have an heir, so his kingdom divided among his four principal generals. The four generals are represented in Daniel's vision as the four heads of the leopard (Dan 7:6). Daniel also depicts the four generals as the four horns of the goat, and he alludes to the generals in non-symbolic language (8:8, 22; 11:4). The kingdom divided as follows:

Figure 7.3. Alexander the Great

Seleucus I Nicator, ruler of Syria and the Levant
Ptolemy I Soter, ruler of Egypt
Cassander, ruler of Greece and Macedonia
Lysimachus, ruler of Thrace and Asia Minor

Of the four generals, only Seleucus and Ptolemy sustained the strength of their kingdoms. The story of the Ptolemaic and Seleucid dynasties comes to bear directly upon the sociopolitical milieu that led up to the time of Jesus Christ. The weak, postexilic Israelites found themselves sandwiched between two powerful empires—the Ptolemies to the south in Egypt, and the Seleucids to the north in Syria.

The Ptolemies and Seleucids

Upon Alexander's death, Ptolemy I seized control of Egypt and ruled there until his death in 282 BC. He is possibly "the king of the south" referred to in Daniel 11:5. Within a few years, Ptolemy extended his control over the land of the Bible. By all appearances, the Jews generally lived in peace as a vassal state of Egypt. This lasted until about 200 BC when the Seleucid king Antiochus III expanded his empire to the south and displaced the Ptolemies by defeating Ptolemy V. The famous Rosetta Stone describes Ptolemy V's ascension to power. Cleopatra, the most famous and final Ptolemaic ruler, exercised power by permission of Rome from 51 BC to 30 BC. She took the wrong side in the Roman civil war following the death of her lover, Julius Caesar. She committed suicide in 30 BC, ending Ptolemaic rule of Egypt.

Antiochus III encouraged divergent religious expression, but his son, Antiochus IV Epiphanes, severely persecuted the Jews. Following a Jewish uprising in 168 BC, Antiochus IV attempted to completely hellenize the Jews by building pagan temples in Jerusalem and forbidding the Jews to practice their religion. The rebellion intensified in 167 BC when Antiochus sacrificed a pig on the altar of the Jerusalem temple and erected a statue of Zeus nearby. Daniel 11:21 and verse 31 possibly allude to Antiochus' desecration of the temple and the events behind "the abomination of desolation." The apocryphal book of 1 Maccabees gives the history of Antiochus' activities. A tetradrachm coin of Antiochus from 167 BC portrays his image on one side, and Zeus' image on the other. The inscription reads,

> Of King Antiochus, god made manifest and victorious

The Hasmonean family secured Jewish independence and rededicated the temple after a forty-two-month war. The Hasmoneans are often referred to as the Maccabees (Hebrew: hammer), a nickname given to Mattathias' eldest son Judas because of his military prowess. The Jewish Feast of Hanukkah, also known as the Feast of Lights or the Feast of Dedication, celebrates the cleansing and rededication of the temple after its defilement by Antiochus IV. Jesus celebrated the Feast of Hanukkah (John 10:22). My team at Khirbet el-Maqatir excavated the coins of Antiochus IV and his successors (fig. 7.4). After

126

Figure 7.4. Silver shekel of Antiochus VII from Khirbet el-Maqatir

regaining independence, the menorah became a major motif in Jewish art. The recently excavated first-century synagogue at Magdala featured a prominently displayed menorah.

Various members of the Hasmonean family ruled Judea for about a century until they acquiesced to the rule of Rome under General Pompey in 63 BC (fig. 7.5). Remnants of Hasmonean rule abound— from coins, to monumental architecture, and so on. Fortresses such as Macherus and Hyrcania were originally built by the Hasmoneans and later rebuilt or fortified by Herod the Great. The royal Hasmonean rulers assumed the roles of king and priest, thus interfering with the Zadokite priesthood that extended back

Figure 7.5. Roman general and prefect Pompey

to the days of the united kingdom. Their interference led to a split within Judaism. A group known as the Essenes withdrew from participation in the Jerusalem Temple and established prophetic communities at wilderness sites such Qumran, ʿEin-Gedi, and Jericho (Pliny, *Natural History* 5.73; Josephus, *Jewish War* 2.119–61). The Essenes also controlled one quarter of Jerusalem in the late Second Temple period. The next chapter expounds upon the Essenes and their writings.

Further Study and Discussion

What synchronisms exist between the book of Nehemiah and the archaeological record?

Why was Cyrus important to the Iron Age IIC period?

What evidence of Cyrus is there in the archaeological record?

What brought about the formation of the group known as the Essenes? What discovery made this group famous in the modern era?

Unreliability of self must be assumed by the interpreter rather than casually attributing such unreliability to the sources available to him. Scarcity of data should never be construed as unreliability.

❖ George Kelm

Chapter 8

The Early Roman Age

In 63 BC, the final Hasmonean ruler, John Hyrcanus, appealed to the Roman general and prefect Pompey for protection in an attempt to avoid domination by Seleucid rule from Syria. Pompey granted protection, but it came at a high cost: the loss of Jewish independence. After the assassination of Julius Caesar, Rome experienced a civil war, with some people favoring Mark Anthony as the next ruler, and others siding with Caesar's adopted son Octavian, later known as Augustus. Everyone in the eastern Mediterranean chose sides.

In a strange twist of fate, an Idumean named Herod—the son of the prominent Antipater—sided with his good friend Mark Anthony. Herod would later name his famous Jerusalem fortress (the Antonia Fortress) after his close friend. Following Anthony's surprising defeat, Herod fled to Rome and convinced Octavian of his loyalty. In 47 BC, Octavian named Herod king or governor over Galilee, and after successfully administering the region, the scope of his reign expanded to include Judea in 40 BC. Within three years his realm expanded to Samaria and Transjordan. As a ruler, Herod distinguished himself as competent but ruthless.

From 37 BC to 1 BC, Herod established himself as the most prolific builder in the world. He designed the amazing seaside city of Caesarea Maritima as an administrative center for Roman rule. This required the construction of a thirty-five-mile-long aqueduct to bring water into the city. A thousand years later, the crusaders scavenged parts of the aqueduct to build their castles, but miles of it still remain even today. Herod also built elegant and massive palaces at Masada, Jericho, Macherus, and many other places. These palaces have all been excavated. Most importantly, Herod rebuilt the Temple and Temple Mount precinct in Jerusalem. He essentially quadrupled the size of the Temple Mount. The retaining walls and surrounding substructure have been largely excavated, and today, the area near the southwest corner of the Temple Mount has an amazing archaeological park administered by the Davidson Center. Jesus was born during the reign of Herod the Great, but Herod died about a year later in extreme pain from an intestinal blockage.

Rome divided Herod's realm among his three surviving sons: Herod Antipas, Herod Phillip, and Herod Archelaus. Herod the Great had killed several of his other sons along with his "beloved" wife Mariamne, a Hasmonean princess. Herod's marriage to Mariamne gave him quasi-legitimacy to rule the Jewish people. When Caesar Augustus learned that Herod had killed his sons, he famously commented, "I would rather be Herod's pig than Herod's son."

Herod Antipas ac-quired the western Gali-lee and Perea. Antipas ordered the decapitation of John the Baptist at Macherus. Macherus, in modern Jordan, has been com-pletely excavated. The excavated area in-cludes the likely place of the holding cell where John was beheaded and the colonnaded plaza area where Salome's dancing led to the execution (fig. 8.1). Opus Sectile paving adorned the plaza, as it did other Herodian struc-tures, including the Temple Mount precincts. In 2016, my colleague

Figure 8.1. Colonnaded area at Macherus where Salome danced

Frankie Snyder published her groundbreaking research on these finely polished geometric pavers.[65]

Just before his crucifixion, Jesus stood trial before Herod Antipas. Antipas built three cities: Tiberias, Sepphoris, and Livias. In 2011, David Graves and I proposed that Tell el-Ḥammam rather than Tell er-Rama is the lost city of Livias.[66] In two other articles, I suggest that the Ephraim of John 11:54 should be located at Khirbet el-Maqatir and not at the traditional site of Taybe.[67] Obviously, archaeology plays a role in identifying cities from the Early Roman Age.

Two other sons of Herod the Great assumed control of the area. Herod Phillip ruled the eastern Galilee, a region equally populated by Jews and gentiles. And Herod Archelaus ruled Judea and Samaria for a decade and built his signature city, named after him-self, in the Jordan Valley, just a few miles north of Jericho. A small portion of Archelaus was excavated, but in recent years looters have ravaged the site. Rome removed Archelaus for incompetence and brutality after he slaughtered three thousand Jews during the Passover of AD 6 in a heavy-handed response to a public disturbance. A Roman prefect or governor replaced him.

Figure 8.2. Pontius Pilate inscription

Four prefects preceded Pontius Pilate, who ruled during the times of Jesus' ministry. Both Josephus and Philo portray Pilate as cruel and capricious. An inscription unearthed at Caesarea in 1961 mentions Pilate and clarifies his title as "prefect" rather than "procurator" (fig. 8.2) The inscription is now on display at the Israel Museum. Pilate was defrocked in AD 36 and recalled to Rome.

Jesus was born during the rule of Augustus Caesar and crucified during the rule of Tiberius Caesar (Luke 2:1). Life-size statues of the two Caesars can be seen in the Vatican Museum in Rome.

One of the most beautiful sites mentioned in the Gospels is Caesarea Philippi (Banias). The name of the site honored Augustus Caesar and Herod Philip. Located at the foot of Mount Hermon, the site is blessed with abundant water from the melted snow. At the time of the New Testament, spring water flowed from a cave adjacent to seven pagan temples. According to Josephus, an earthquake in AD 66 redirected the water from the Cave of Pan to a nearby tributary. The Greeks viewed the cave as entrance to the underworld. The temples, all excavated in the twentieth century, glorified pagan deities such as Pan (the god of nature), Zeus (the god of war), the goat-dancing gods, and Caesar. A huge boulder sat in front of the temples and potentially provided visual reinforcement to Jesus' statement in Matthew 16:18, "Upon this rock I will build my church, and the gates of hell will not prevail against it." The "gates of hell" possibly referred to the seven pagan temples. A similar statement in Revelation 2:12, "I know that you dwell where Satan's throne is," might allude to the great altar of Pergamon which is now in the Pergamon Museum in Berlin.[68] A massive frieze of cosmic battles between giants and the Greek gods encircled the altar.

The Architecture at Capernaum

The village of Capernaum, located on the northern shore of the Sea of Galilee, features some of the most impressive ruins in the Galilee. Capernaum and nearby Bethsaida were the dual headquarters for Jesus' ministry. Herod Antipas ruled Capernaum, while Herod Phillip controlled Bethsaida. Jesus moved between the two jurisdictions in response to the political tensions that resulted from his ministry.

Two structures from Capernaum interest students of biblical archaeology. One of them is a synagogue. The remains of the synagogue now standing are from the fourth century, but the clearly visible basalt foundation certainly belongs to the synagogue of Jesus' day (Luke 7:1–10).[69] The early dating is reliable, regardless of the protest of Jodi Magness and a handful of likeminded archaeologists.

The second structure of importance is a residential home, possibly even the home of Peter, where at least two miracles occurred. Archaeology has confirmed that the house functioned as an early house church. Later builders erected different church structures over it. The most recent one, the octagonal church, greets visitors today. A modern church superstructure now protects the important ruins.

The Ritual Purity Movement

Late in the Second Temple period, around 100 BC, a wave of ritual purity swept through Judaism. It remains unclear just what set off this seismic movement, but a number of changes in the material culture reflect its influence. The cultural changes include (a) secondary burials in limestone ossuaries, (b) the use of stone vessels, and (c) the daily practice of immersion in the waters of a mikvah.

Ossuary Burials

Simple trench graves, like the thousand or so found at Khirbet Qumran, served the burial needs of many peasants and criminals. However, secondary burials in limestone ossuaries gained widespread popularity among the upper and middle classes in Palestine. Artisans exclusively utilized limestone ossuaries. In accord with the funerary custom of the day, one would place the corpse in a rock-hewn and ventilated tomb for one year, during which time the body would decay, leaving only the bones (fig. 8.3). The bones would then be collected and placed in an ossuary. Ossuaries were typically twenty inches long, twelve inches high, and ten inches wide. The next family member to decease would undergo the same process in the same tomb.

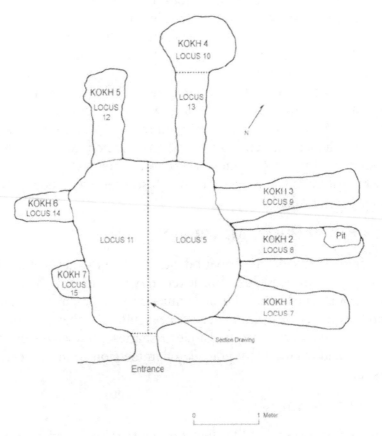

Figure 8.3. First-century tomb at Khirbet el-Maqatir

Thousands of ossuaries have been found, many with inscriptions (fig. 8.4). For example, in the 1950s, at Dominus Flevit on the Mount of Olives, the great Italian archaeologist

Bellarmino Bagatti discovered hundreds of ossuaries, some with what appears to be Christian iconography.

Since 1990, two extremely important ossuaries have surfaced. One of them was an ornate ossuary dating to the first century AD. It originated in a burial cave in the wealthy priestly sector of Jerusalem. The ossuary bore an inscription indicating that it was the final resting place of the bones of Joseph Caiaphas, the high priest who was complicit in the illegal execution of Jesus. The tomb of Caiaphas' father-in-law Annas sits a short distance south of the pool of Siloam.

In 2002, another ossuary came to light. It contained a brief Hebrew inscription that shook the world:

James, son of Joseph, brother of Jesus

Figure 8.4. Ossuary, first century AD

A firestorm of controversy surrounds this simple bone box and its inscription. Many scholars such as André Lemaire vouch for its authenticity. Lemaire was the world's leading epigraphist and chairman of the Department of Hebrew and Aramaic Philology and Epigraphy at the Paris-Sorbonne University. Wolfgang Krumbein, a world-renowned expert in stone chemistry and biology, corroborated Lemaire's assessment. If authentic, the ossuary constitutes the oldest extrabiblical mention of Jesus and his family members. Many other voices, though, including the Israel Antiquities Authority, believe that all or part of the inscription is a forgery. Forgeries plague the field of archaeology.

James, the brother of Jesus, assumed the leadership of the nascent Jesus movement after the execution of his older brother. Eventually, the temple establishment murdered James, according to the fourth-century church historian Eusebius, who derived his information from the second-century writer Hegesippus (ca. AD 180). After beating James with clubs, the religious leaders threw him off the pinnacle of the temple (Eusebius, *Ecclesiastical History* 2.23). Eusebius also mentions that James was buried nearby, south of the temple, exactly where the James Ossuary likely originated.

The only other time in history that ossuaries were used was during the Chalcolithic Age, prior to the patriarchal era. The clay Chalcolithic ossuaries often portrayed anthropoid shapes.

Archaeology exposes the contrast between the values of Christianity and the pagan Roman Empire. From the first century AD to the collapse of the empire in the fifth century, many Romans marked their graves with the inscription *nffnsnc*. Scholars eventually deciphered the Latin: *non fui non sum non curo*, "I was not, I was, I am not, I do not care." Their apathetic outlook contrasts radically with the Christian epitaphs in the catacombs, which express joy in the present life and hope for eternity. Craig Evans devotes the final chapter of his book *Jesus and the Remains of His Day* to the stark contrast between Pagan epithets and Judeo-Christian epitaphs. According to him, "In a sense, through these inscriptions the dead can talk to the living."[70]

Stone Vessels

Around the same time that funerary practices changed, the Jewish population of Palestine began using stone vessels as a means of maintaining ritual purity (fig. 8.5). These soft and chalky limestone vessels only appear at Jewish sites in the late Second Temple period. Apparently, the Jews saw stone vessels as a way around the Mosaic law, which required pottery to be broken

Figure 8.5. Stone cup from Khirbet el-Maqatir, first century AD

once it became impure (Lev 11:33–35; 15:12). Impurity could be caused by (a) exposure to a bodily excretion, such as spit, (b) the presence of mold or mildew, or (c) physical contact with an unclean per-son, such as woman during her menstrual cycle or some-one who had touched a corpse within the week.

Stone vessel factories operated from Jerusalem to the Galilee. Shimon Gibson identified a large factory at Hizma, five miles north of Jerusalem. Yitzhak Magen excavated the factory and published his findings. Clearly, the factories produced the larger lathe-formed vessels, but it seems likely that the artisans from surrounding villages purchased chunks of limestone from the factories and produced smaller vessels in their own local workshops or homes.

At most Jewish sites, the presence of stoneware in the early first century BC coincides with the absence of the fancy and popular eastern terra sigillata ware. Jews rejected foreign influence in favor of locally made wares. The water that Jesus turned to wine filled stone jars, not clay jars (John 2:6–10).

Ritual Immersions

Along with secondary burial and the adoption of stone vessels, Jews also began the ubiquitous practice of ritual immersion in water. A mikvah (plural: mikvaot) was normally carved into bedrock (living stone) and filled with running water (living water). Male and female devotees would disrobe, descended the steps (usually seven), and immerse themselves.

At Qumran, the Essenes practiced ritual immersion multiple times per day. In light of this, it is no surprise that three thousand people experienced baptism on the day of Pentecost. But, they had never before experienced baptism in the name of Jesus.

Archaeologists have documented more than one thousand mikvaot in Israel. Fewer exist per capita in the Galilee where the Sea of Galilee served as a massive public mikvah. Khirbet Nisya, Khirbet el-Maqatir, and Shiloh, three sites excavated by the Associates for Biblical Research, all had ritual immersion baths from the late Second Temple period.

Archaeology and the Book of Acts

Like the rest of the Bible, archaeology sheds light on the book of Acts. Due to the historical nature of Acts, the book contains numerous synchronisms.

Proconsul Sergius Paulus

Two inscriptions dating to the mid-first century have been found at Cyprus. They refer to a proconsul by the name of Paulus or Sergius Paulus. Saul convinced the proconsul to convert to Christianity on his first missionary journey (Acts 13:6–12). Some interpreters suggest that Saul changed his name to Paul in honor of this man. Regardless, from Acts 13 and onward, the writer of the book refers to the apostle as Paul, a more common and acceptable name in gentile culture. The name Saul was more acceptable to Jews, and it remained as a classic Jewish name since the time of Israel's first king.

Proconsul Gallio

The Jewish community persecuted Paul at Corinth. They brought him before Gallio who dismissed the case before Paul could even provide a defense (Acts 18:12–17). A letter from the emperor Cladius, found at Delphi, Greece, provides a concrete dating of Paul's eighteen months at Corinth. The letter itself dates to AD 50–52. One snippet of the letter reads,

> Lucius Junius Gallio, my friend, and the proconsul of Achaia.

Gallio's younger brother, Seneca, tutored and advised Nero, the successor of Claudius. Seneca deserves credit for the peace during the first five years of Nero's reign. But after Nero's twenty-third birthday, he banished Seneca and began his infamous reign of terror.

Jesus and His Brother James

The first-century historian Josephus verifies many people and events of the book of Acts in his monumental works, *Jewish Antiquities* and the *Jewish War*. Six non-Christian literary sources from the first or early second centuries of the Christian era refer to Jesus:

1. Josephus, who also mentions James, the brother of Jesus (Jewish Antiquities 18.3.3; 20.9.1)
2. Tacitus (Annals 15.44.3)
3. Pliny the Younger (Epistles 10.96–97)
4. Suetonius (Claudius 25.4; Nero 16.2)
5. James Ossuary (potentially authentic)
6. Incantation bowls

First-century exorcists wrote Aramaic spells inside ceramic bowls. Several of these incantation bowls mention Jesus of Nazareth among other deities, thus indicating an awareness of the person of Jesus.[71]

Discoveries concerning Ephesus

From 1863 to 1874, British archaeologist John Wood completely excavated Ephesus and confirmed many of the features mentioned in Acts 19. Most importantly, Wood uncovered the Temple of Artemis (the Temple of Diana), one of the seven wonders of the ancient world. The Ephesus Archaeological Museum in Turkey displays many images of the famous Greco-Roman goddess. Likewise, Wood revealed the twenty-five thousand seat theater (fig. 8.6). At the theater, a riot broke out because idol sales had plummeted as a result of the preaching of the gospel (Acts 19:23).

Figure 8.6. Theater at Ephesus

An inscription found at Corinth in 1929 names Erastus (Acts 19:22; Rom 16:23; 2 Tim 4:20). The inscription reads as follows:

> Erastus in return for his aedileship [administrative position] paved it [entrance to the theater] at his own expense.

The Erastus of this inscription likely corresponds to the Erastus of Acts and Paul's letters. A separate tradition holds that Erastus was one of the seventy (or seventy-two) disciples sent out by Jesus (Luke 10:1–23).

Discoveries concerning Athens

Most of the breathtaking edifices and features of ancient Athens have been excavated and restored, including the Parthenon and Mars Hill. Although the inscription "To an Unknown God" mentioned in Acts 17:23 has not yet been found, the very same inscription was discovered at Pergamon, thus establishing the existence of such a belief system at the time of Paul's journeys.

The First Jewish Revolt

In AD 66, the Jews finally attempted to overthrow their Roman occupiers. Their ill-fated attempt lasted three and a half years. It resulted in the death of a million Jews and the enslavement of one hundred thousand more. Josephus describes the final phase of the Roman response to the revolt:

> Caesar, finding it impracticable to reduce the upper city without earthworks, owing to the precipitous nature of the site, on the twentieth of the month Lous [Ab] apportioned the task among his forces. The conveyance of timber was, however, arduous, all the environs of the city to a distance of a hundred furlongs having, as I said, been stripped bare…. The earthworks having now been completed after eighteen days' labor, on the seventh of the month Gorpiaeus [Elul], the Romans brought up the engines. Of the rebels, some already despairing of the city retired from the ramparts to the citadel, others slunk down into the tunnels. Pouring into the alleys, sword in hand, they [the Romans] massacred indiscriminately all whom they met, and burnt the houses with all who had taken refuge within. Often in the course of their raids, on entering the houses for loot, they would find whole families dead and

the rooms filled with the victims of the famine ...
Running everyone through who fell in their way,
they choked the alleys with corpses and deluged the
whole city with blood, insomuch that many of the
fires were extinguished by the gory stream. Towards
evening they ceased slaughtering, but when night
fell the fire gained the mastery, and the dawn of the
eighth day of the month Gorpiaeus [Elul] broke
upon Jerusalem in flames—a city which had
suffered such calamities ... The Romans now set
fire to the outlying quarters of the town and razed
the walls to the ground. Thus was Jerusalem taken
in the second year of the reign of Vespasian, on the
eighth of the month Gorpiaeus [20 September, 70
A.D.]. (*Jewish War* 6.8–10)

In August of AD 70, Jerusalem finally fell to the Roman prince
and future emperor Titus.[72] The temple and its associated
structures suffered destruction, and the Romans looted the temple
treasury. Although Titus ordered the soldiers of the Tenth Legion
not to burn the temple, they disobeyed, resulting in the gold
melting down between the paving stones. In order to retrieve the
gold, the soldiers plowed up the stones on the Temple Mount,
perhaps fulfilling the prophecy that Zion would be plowed as a
field (Mic 3:12). The temple burned on about August 28th, and the
rest of the city fell violently on about September 20th. The
cessation of the sacrificial system ended traditional Judaism and
began rabbinic Judaism. The western Galilee town of Sepphoris, a
short distance from Nazareth, became the center of the new
rabbinic Judaism.

Many Bible interpreters see the war as a partial or complete
fulfillment of Jesus' Olivet Discourse (Matt 24–25; Mark 13; Luke
21). A plethora of archaeological evidence establishes this war.
Some of the more notable evidences include the following items.

The Temple Mount

When the Romans razed the Temple Mount, they took the ashlars from the temple buildings and pushed them off the southwest corner of the Temple Mount platform. Even today many of the ashlars remain in situ, although some have been removed so that tourists can see the street below. Coins found below the street date to the year AD 66, just prior to the beginning of the revolt. An inscription discovered at the southwest corner of the temple refers to the trumpeter who signaled the beginning and end of the Sabbath. The inscription reads as follows:

> The Place of the Trumpeter

Figure 8.7. Gentile prohibition

A different inscription confirms that the temple authorities prohibited the gentiles from entering the inner court (fig. 8.7). Jewish leaders falsely accused the apostle Paul of violating the boundary by bringing Trophimus the Ephesian (a Greek) into the inner court (Acts 21:27–36). Ephesians 2:14 possibly alludes to the wall of separation. The inscription reads,

> No foreigner is allowed to enter the balustrade
> surrounding the sanctuary and the enclosed court.
> Whoever is caught will be responsible for his own
> death.

Josephus mentions both inscriptions (*Jewish War* 5.2.2). The inscriptions are currently in the Istanbul Archaeological Museum.[73]

The Tenth Roman Legion

The Tenth Roman Legion suppressed the First Jewish Revolt. The revolt culminated in the burning of the temple on the ninth of Ab (August 28th). In 587 BC, the Babylonians destroyed the First Temple on the same day of the year. The timing provided an unmistakable sign of divine judgment.

After the destruction of the Jewish nation, Vespasian stationed the Tenth Legion at Jerusalem in the Old City, near Mount Zion. They remained in the area through the Second Jewish Revolt (AD 132–135), which they mercilessly crushed. During times of peace, the legion engaged in civil service projects, such as building aqueducts or paving public walkways. They developed their own workshops and produced building materials such as ceiling tiles. Their materials were stamped with the seal of their legion: *legio x fretensis*, "the Tenth Legion of the Straight," or *lxf* for short. Evidences of their occupation are ubiquitous.

The Burnt House

In 1970, Nahman Avigad excavated a wealthy Jerusalem home from the first century AD. The home had been destroyed and burned by the Romans. Avigad documented a number of coins at floor level. Some Roman coins bore the images of various procurators, but most belonged to the upstart Jewish state. The Jewish coins were inscribed as follows: "year two, the freedom of Zion" and "year three, the freedom of Zion" and "year four, the redemption of Zion." A spear was among the excavated objects. It likely belonged to the owner of the house. Today, the restored and impressive archaeological site educates visitors in underground

Jerusalem.[74] Interestingly, the house likely rests upon the ruins of houses from the First Temple period.

The First-Century Coins

Excavations have yielded thousands of coins dating to the first century AD. After the First Revolt, Rome issued a special coin bearing the inscription "Judea Capta," "Judah is captive." Every time a Jew made a financial transaction, the coin re-minded him of his status as captive or slave. The obverse side of the coin

Figure 8.8. *Judea Capta* coin

shows a Jewish slave under a palm tree under the watchful eye of a Roman overlord (fig. 8.8). The date palm, rare in the modern Levant, grew prolifically in Bible times, particularly along the Jordan River and the northern shore of the Dead Sea.

The Arch of Titus

A triumphal arch still stands in Rome on the *Via Sacra* (sacred road). It commemorates Titus' defeat of the Jews. The interior of the arch depicts the Romans carrying the plunder from the temple, including the seven-branched menorah. It also shows Titus at the head of a triumphal procession, accompanied by the goddesses Victoria and Roma (cp. 2 Cor 2:14; fig. 8.9).

The Roman Coliseum

The riches from the Jerusalem temple financed the construction of the famous coliseum that still stands in Rome. Jewish slaves from

Jerusalem and throughout Judea provided the construction labor. Vespasian began the project, and Titus completed it. Hence, the most famous building in Rome bears witness to the First Jewish Revolt.

Figure 8.9. Arch of Titus

The Dead Sea Scrolls

In 1947, a young shepherd made the most important archaeological discovery of the twentieth century. In a cave near the northwest edge of the Dead Sea, he found several clay jars that contained ancient parchments. Many of these textual fragments included portions of the Old Testament. An exhaustive search of the caves in the area yielded one library of biblical and sectarian scrolls. The scrolls, dating from the second century BC to AD 68, predate the oldest extant biblical Hebrew manuscripts by about a thousand years. The Essenes likely wrote the Dead Sea Scrolls. This apocalyptic sect withdrew from participation in the Jerusalem temple after the Hasmoneans usurped the office of the priest, thus disrupting the unbroken Zadokite service since the time of David.

The Romans destroyed the Qumran community in AD 68. Some refugees fled to Masada, as evidenced by the scroll fragments found there. Today, the scrolls reside in various locations, such as the Shrine of the Book in Jerusalem, the Jordan Archaeological Museum in Amman, the museums throughout the western world, and even the collections of private individuals.

The discovery of the Dead Sea Scrolls revolutionized textual scholarship. Fragments of every biblical book except Esther came from the caves, along with biblical commentaries and other sectarian scrolls, such as the War Scroll, the Thanksgiving Scroll, and the Rule of the Community (Serek Hayahad). An excerpt from the Thanksgiving Scroll provides a glimpse into the values of the fascinating Essene community:

> As for me, I know that righteousness belongs not to a human being, nor perfection of way to a son of man. To God Most High belong all the deeds of righteousness, whereas the path of a human is not set firm... (1QH IV, 30–38)

While there is not a direct connection that links the literature of the Qumran community with early Christianity, numerous similarities indicate a closely related belief system. The four examples below illustrate the commonalities.

The Apocryphon of Daniel (4Q246). This text from Cave 4 consists of two columns of Aramaic text. It dates to the late first century BC. The text refers to "the Son of the Most High" and "the Son of God." Luke 1:31–35 also employs those phrases. Likewise, Acts 16:17 reads, "These men are servants of the Most High God."

The Messianic Apocalypse (4Q521). This script, also from Cave 4, states that "When Messiah appears, heaven and earth will obey him. He will lift up the downtrodden and heal the injured. The dead will be raised, and the poor will hear the good news." The wording resembles the words of Jesus: "The blind receive sight. The lame walk, those who have leprosy are cleansed, the deaf hear, the dead are raised, the good news is proclaimed to the poor" (Luke 7:22).

The Melchizedek Scroll (11Q13). This Cave 11 excerpt teaches that Melchizedek will return in fulfillment of Isaiah 61:1–3, "The Spirit of the Sovereign LORD is on me because the LORD has anointed me." This mirrors Luke 4:18–19, which states, "The Spirit of the Lord is upon me because he has anointed me."

The War Scroll (1QM). This script from Cave 1 dates to the turn of the century, around the birth of Christ. It describes a forty-nine-year war between the sons of light and darkness. The language is almost identical to the observation by Jesus: "people of

Figure 8.10. Excavation of Cave 12; *left to right*, Randall Price, Scott Stripling, and David Graves

the world are more shrewd in dealing with their own kind than the people of the light" (Luke 16:8; cf. John 12:26).

For the past two generations, scholars assumed that the scrolls came from only eleven caves. That assumption changed in January 2017 when a joint expedition from Hebrew University and Liberty University excavated a new cave containing broken scroll jars and associated objects. Sadly, modern looters had already reached the cave, and only one scrap of parchment escaped their scrutiny. I was in Israel at the time of the discovery and was invited by the excavators to be among the first to see what is now referred to as Cave 12 (fig. 8.10).

The Desert Fortress

For all practical purposes, the war ended in AD 70 when Jerusalem fell. However, the final group of rebels held out until AD 73. The rebels were called *Sicarii* (knife men). They found refuge in Herod's desert stronghold, known simply as Masada (fortress). In order to breach the fortress walls, the Romans used Jewish slaves to build an earthen siege ramp, which remains even today. To avoid capture and enslavement, the rebels (almost one thousand of them) killed their own families, and then cast lots to determine the order in which they would kill one another (Josephus, *Jewish War* 4.7.2). An ostracon found in the Masada synagogue bore the name of the group's leader, Eleazar ben Yair. Masada serves as perhaps the most spectacular archaeological site in Israel (fig. 8.11).[75]

The Second Jewish Revolt

Even after the catastrophic failure of the First Jewish Revolt, many Jews continued to fan the flames of the nationalistic movement. Hopes of rebuilding the temple and achieving political independence reached a crescendo in AD 132. The renowned Rabbi Akiva had persuaded the Sanhedrin to accept Simon Bar Kokhba as the messiah and to back the revolt. But by AD 135, the Romans had crushed the movement. It ended in tragedy for the Jews, much like the ending of the First Revolt. Another half million Jews died in addition to the one million killed in the First Jewish Revolt. When taken together, the numbers represent a greater percentage of Jewish deaths than the holocaust of World War II. The devastating losses of the First and Second Jewish Revolts might confirm the prophecy of Jesus in Matthew 24:21, "there will be great suffering, such as has not been from the beginning of the world until now, no, and never will be."

Figure 8.11. Approach to Masada

Abundant evidence of the Second Jewish Revolt populates the archaeological record. Let us consider some of the evidence.

The Cave of Letters

In 1960, archaeologists found fifteen letters in a cave at Naḥal Ḥever, overlooking the western side of the Dead Sea. The letters were written by Bar Kokhba, the leader or messianic figure of the revolt. He wrote to his officers at ʿEin-Gedi, about five miles north. The following year, archaeologists unearthed yet another set of correspondences from the same cave. These scripts became known as the Babatha letters. They belonged to a Jewish woman named Babatha who was living as a refugee in the cave in order to escape the Romans. The letters greatly enhance our understanding of the role and status of women in the second century. They also shed light on the leader of the Second Revolt.

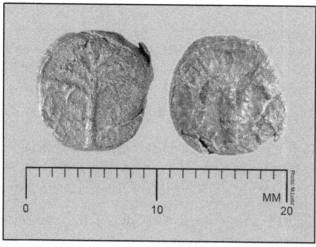

Figure 8.12. Coin of Bar Kokhba from Khirbet el-Maqatir

The Revolt Coins

As one of their first acts, the rebels minted their own coins. The coins display an image of the temple on one side, indicating their intent to rebuild the temple. The coins bear the stamp of years one through four of the short-lived uprising. The words "freedom" and "redemption" appear on many of the coins. Bar Kokhba coins rarely come to light from controlled excavations. Most appear on the antiquities market as the result of the illegal plundering of sites. Figure 8.12 shows a coin that was excavated in a hiding complex at Khirbet el-Maqatir.

The Colony Aelia Capitolina

After the destruction of Jerusalem, only three towers built by Herod the Great remained standing: Hippicus, Phasael, and Mariamne. Titus left them intact in order to show what a great city he had conquered. At the conclusion of the Second Jewish Revolt, the emperor Hadrian leveled the towers and any rebuilt structures. On top of the ruins he built a classic Greco-Roman city that he named Aelia Capitolina. Excavations revealed the cardo (main street) of this second-century city. The Romans minted Aelia Capitolina coins in AD 132. They also built temples to Jupiter and Venus at the site of the former Jewish temple and the place of the crucifixion and resurrection of Jesus.

The Fragmentary Textual Evidence

The New Testament authors inscribed their autographs (documents) on papyrus. The autographs were read and reread, copied and recopied. Eventually, the originals simply fell apart. In recent decades, however, fragments of ancient copies have resurfaced. One such fragment, discovered in Egypt, includes John 18:31–33 and verses 37–38. It dates to the late first or early second century, making it the oldest extant New Testament fragment. Known as P52, it currently belongs in the extensive John Rylands collection.

Craig Evans and a cadre of other scholars have identified what appears to be fragments of Mark's Gospel among some papier-mâché Egyptian death masks from the first century. Their cutting-edge research holds tremendous potential for textual scholarship. Furthermore, infrared technology may soon enable scholars to read the carbonized library of scrolls from Herculaneum, the sister city of Pompey that was buried by the eruption of Mount Vesuvius in AD 79.

Further Study and Discussion

How did Herod the Great come to power? What significant things did he build?

What archaeological evidence is there of the destruction of Jerusalem in AD 70 and the subsequent destruction in AD 135?

What extrabiblical sources from the first and second centuries refer to Jesus?

What technologies hold great promise for textual scholarship?

Where there are two archaeologists, there are three opinions.

❖ Anonymous

Chapter 9

The Byzantine Age

The Byzantine Age in Palestine extended from the Council of Nicaea in AD 325 to the crushing loss at the hands of the upstart Muslim armies at the battle of the Yarmuk in AD 636. Within one year of the battle, the entire Holy Land fell into Muslim hands. The Byzantine Empire continued, but it lost size and power.

Constantine's Influence upon Christianity

Constantine's apparent conversion in AD 312 changed Christianity. Americans talk about "the Jacksonian age" to summarize the enormous impact of the eighth president, Andrew Jackson, on the development of the country. Similarly, but even more profoundly, Christians talk about "the age of Constantine" to characterize the enormous impact that his conversion had on the Christian church and on Roman society generally.

Were the societal changes that emanated from Constantine positive, negative, or a combination of both? The Eastern Church saw Constantine as "The initiator of the Christian world, the instrument of the victory of light over darkness."[76] The Western Church, on the other hand, viewed Constantine's initiatives as "The beginning of the enslavement of the church by the state."[77] Eusebius' *Onomasticon* and *Ecclesiastical History* shed light on the controversial role of Constantine at the Council of Nicaea.

In the early fourth century, a political upheaval ensued. Diocletian shocked the empire by his abdication in AD 305. Before his abdication, he initiated a plan of succession that involved two sub-emperors, one ruling in the east and the other in the west. Galerius ruled in the east, and Constantine's father and Maximian, who had ruled jointly with Diocletian, ruled in the west. In AD 306, Constantine Jr. succeeded his father and eventually conquered Maximian, forcing him to commit suicide. Maxentius, the son of Maximian, did not take the news well, and he went on to challenge Constantine for rule in the west. The challenge culminated in the famous battle at the Milvian Bridge in AD 312. At that battle, Constantine allegedly converted to Christianity.

In the previous year, AD 311, Galerius had died of a horrible disease, perhaps cancer of the bowels, which Eusebius described in detail. Galerius had been complicit in the persecution of Christians by Diocletian. Before Galerius died, he issued the Edict of Toleration that made life more tolerable for believers. With Galerius dead and Maximian and Maxentius defeated, the empire had a ruler who favored Christianity. Table 9.1 displays a basic timeline for the development of Christianity.

Table 9.1. Timeline of early and medieval Christianity

30–313	Christianity characterized by persecution and growth
313–380	Christianity characterized by toleration, acceptance, and peace
380–395	Christianity prevails under Theodosius
395–1100s	Christianity advocated by the state

Much like the Cyrus Cylinder from the Persian era, the Edict of Milan (AD 313) assured the free practice of religion. The edict states,

> When I, Constantine Augustus, as well as I, Licinius Augustus, fortunately met near Milan, and were considering everything that pertained to the public welfare and security, we thought, among other things which we saw would be for the good of many, those regulations pertaining to the reverence of the Divinity ought certainly to be made first, so that we might grant to the Christians and others full authority to observe that religion which each preferred; whence any Divinity whatsoever in the seat of the heavens may be propitious and kindly

disposed to us and all who are placed under our rule.

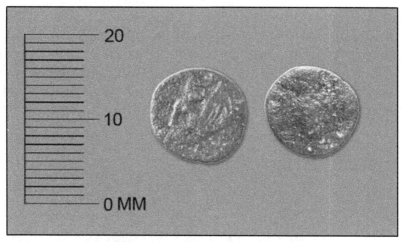

Figure 9.1. Coin of Theodosius I from Khirbet el-Maqatir

Eusebius and many other Christians were ecstatic, but not everyone shared their optimism. Authorities returned church property that had been confiscated, and they paid reparations. In addition, the government allocated funds to build worship centers and pay the salaries of ministers. Soldiers provided protection. Constantine held a reception banquet, and three hundred bishops attended. The clergy obtained tax-exemption and became privileged. Ecclesiastical trials enjoyed sanction, and new laws ended the brutal practice of crucifixion and greatly reduced infanticide. Slavery became more humane, and gladiatorial games mostly ceased.

In Rome, the number of Christians grew from thirty thousand in AD 250 to three hundred thousand in AD 340. In the year 380, the great preacher, John "Golden Mouth" Chrysostom, noted the presence of one-hundred thousand believers in Antioch, which amounted to half the population. Christians were no longer seen as weird.

The tables turned under Theodosius the Great, the last ruler of east *and* west (cf. fig. 9.1). Churches inherited endowments held by pagan temples. The famous words of Tertullian finally rang true: "We are but of yesterday, yet we already fill your cities, your islands, forts, towns; we have left you only your temples" (Tertullian, *Plea for Allegiance* A.2). The state forbade non-Christian sacrifices and abolished the death penalty for idol worshippers. Censorship of anti-Christian books became the norm. People were not permitted to write or speak against Christianity. The persecuted became the persecutors.

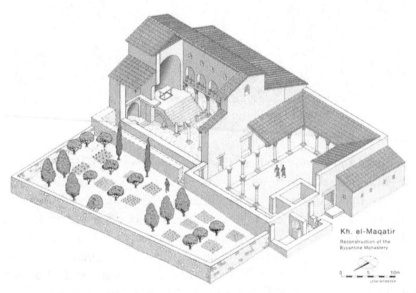

Figure 9.2. Monastery at Khirbet el-Maqatir

The archaeology of the Byzantine Age reflects indirectly upon the biblical text. And certainly, it is instructive for a fuller understanding of church history. For example, the fourth- to sixth-century church and monastery at Khirbet el-Maqatir yielded first-century ossuary fragments in secondary usage and abundant coins from the biblical era (fig. 9.2). I excavated the church and monastery between 2010 and 2016. The dimensions of the Khirbet el-Maqatir church mirror the dimensions of Solomon's Temple, with a ratio of two to one, of holy space to most holy space.

The new policies of toleration set off a pilgrimage industry and a demographic shift. The Holy Land reached its greatest population density until the nineteenth century. The Byzantine period produced great church leaders—often called the post-Nicene fathers—such as Chrysostom, Eusebius, Jerome, Ambrose, and Augustine.

During the Byzantine era, some of Christianity's earliest structures were built for religious activity in the Holy Land. Although postbiblical, they contribute greatly to biblical studies by helping to identify and preserve the locations, names, and traditions of numerous biblical sites. One such structure, St. George's Church in Madaba, has a sixth-century mosaic on the floor. The mosaic is known as the Madaba Map (fig. 9.3). At Shiloh, one of the four Byzantine churches there has intact mosaics that actually contain the name Shiloh.

Figure 9.3. Madaba Map, sixth century

Where Christians Gathered

In the New Testament period, churches were primarily associated with houses (Rom 16:5; 1 Cor 16:19; Col 4:15; Phlm 2). Archaeologists have unearthed a few "house churches" (Latin: *domus ecclesiae*). One such example from Capernaum is Peter's house-turned-shrine with a later Byzantine church built above it (cf. Mark 1:29). It appears to have been a typical house from a village of the first century AD. It included several buildings inside a walled compound. It became a shrine prior to construction of the octagonal Byzantine church above the remains of the house. During the third century AD, a Roman-style house turned into a church was found in Dura-Europos, along the Euphrates River in Syria. The modest nature of this house church suggests that the congregation lacked demographic and financial resources.

Unlike later churches, these house churches originally functioned as homes. Later, believers converted them into churches for public worship. Prior to Constantine, very few structures were built specifically for public worship. However, two recently excavated churches reveal that during lulls of persecution in the third century some buildings were constructed uniquely for Christian worship. In 1995, Yotam Tepper excavated a church at Kefar Othnay near Megiddo that dates to about AD 230.[78] Likewise, a late third-century worship center was unearthed in 1998 at Aqaba, Jordan.[79] Churches were also erected in Tyre and Rome (ca. AD 315).

During the Byzantine period, Christianity underwent a dramatic change. As an official religion throughout the Roman Empire, it prospered under special encouragement by Constantine. Major religious architectural projects were undertaken around the Mediterranean. At least three churches were constructed in Rome, but church construction was particularly accelerated in the Holy Land.

Beginning in AD 326, Constantine and his mother Helena constructed four churches in Palestine at places of christological significance: the Church of the Nativity in Bethlehem, the Church of the Holy Sepulchre in Jerusalem, the Church of Eleona on the Mount of Olives (the ascension site), and the church at Mamre (Hebron), the site of the christophany in Genesis 18:1. With royal encouragement, additional churches that commemorated Old and New Testament holy places were soon constructed throughout the country.

The plan of the familiar Roman civic building served as the blueprint for churches. The building was called a "basilica" and used for public, private, and sacred purposes. Basilicas had a rectangular central hall (nave), rows of interior pillar roof supports, side aisles, a raised platform (chancel), and an apse. Churches constructed in the basilica style regularly placed the apse on the east and a triple main entrance on the west. Later, Byzantine basilica-style churches added two extra apses, totaling three on the east.

Some churches commemorated holy locations, while others were more utilitarian and served the communal needs of Christians in a given area. Emphasizing the structure's center, these churches were built on circular, octagonal, square or cruciform plans. The Byzantine church over Peter's house and the Church of the Kathisma outside Bethlehem are examples of octagonal churches.

In the Byzantine period, bishops encouraged the construction of more elaborate structures befitting the faith's new status. Outwardly, these structures continued to be modest in appearance, while inside they became quite ornate, fulfilling the royal urgings.

After construction of the original large Constantinian churches, most builders in Palestine constructed small and modest churches. Designed to serve rural and urban congregations as well as monasteries, virtually every village had a church by the end of the Byzantine period, and many towns had more than one. Five churches have been excavated at the decapolis city of Abila in northern Jordan.

In addition to the construction of churches in the Holy Land, monasteries were also popular in the region. In the Judean desert, they served as homes for monks living under vows and as hostels for visiting pilgrims. Euthymius founded the monastic movement, and the well-preserved monastery bearing his name can be visited on the south side of the Dead Sea highway, about halfway between Jerusalem and Jericho. The first monasteries benefitted a community of recluses who lived in isolation during the week and met for common prayer on weekends. The recluses settled near mountain cliffs, caves, and natural rock cover near settlements. A monastery that housed monks in their own cells or caves away from the central chapel was called a "path" (Greek: *laura*), named for the path leading from the cells to the chapel.

In the late fifth century AD, the *coenobium*-type monastery became popular. *Coenobium* (Latin: "communal life") monasteries were usually surrounded by a perimeter and included a chapel, refectory, sleeping quarters, service areas, atrium, and even a hostel for visiting pilgrims. Monks lived and worked together daily.

In summary, the Byzantines of Palestine were industrious. Unfortunately, they often ruled in a heavy-handed manner in their administration of Palestine, leading to several Samaritan revolts of the fifth and sixth centuries. Many churches were destroyed during these revolts. While all the remains from the Byzantine period do not represent religious activity or even religious people, the region was filled with churches, monasteries, monks, and pilgrims who were seriously interested in biblical things. Those indefatigable Byzantines continued to thrive in Palestine well into the early Islamic era. We are indebted to them for the landmarks that they left across the Holy Land.

With the Muslim victory over Emperor Heraclius and the Christian forces at the battle of the Yarmuk, the Byzantine era in Palestine closed, and the Early Islamic era began. Christians once again learned how to live under persecution.[80]

Further Study and Discussion

What brought about the end of the persecution of Christians?

What edicts document the change of policy regarding Christians?

Why is the Madaba Map important?

What is the significance of the battle of the Yarmuk?

Conclusion

God left two great witnesses of his work of redemption in history—the Bible and the physical remains of ancient cultures. However, only a small percentage of the physical remains of the ancient world have survived (in a form recognizable to us). Many centuries have passed since the remains were originally constructed, carved, written, and so forth. Of those that survive, only a small percentage have been excavated. Surprisingly, only about 5 percent of the physical remains in the Levant have been excavated. Nonetheless, we live in the golden age of archaeology. The last century yielded more inscriptions and artifacts than the previous six thousand years of recorded history. Walter Rast writes,

> Even though archaeology deals with age-old things that have been covered over by soil and debris for centuries, it has only been in recent times that methods have been developed for retrieving this valuable information. Archaeology is a very young field of investigation, but in its brief existence it has transformed our thinking about people and cultures in most parts of the world. So young is it that it is possible to say that the birth of modern Palestinian archaeology occurred little more than 100 years ago.[81]

The next century will be mind boggling in the discoveries that it yields. Will the archive be unearthed at Hazor or Shiloh? Will future inscriptions prove Israel's establishment in Canaan in the fourteenth century BC? Only time will tell.

The fragile peace of the region makes future projects tentative. Terrorist organizations such as Hamas in the Gaza Strip and the Islamic State in Iraq and Syria (ISIS) actively target antiquities. The two world wars of the twentieth century shut down archaeological work for years. Wars can result in the looting of irreplaceable antiquities in museums and universities. The overthrow of the Iraqi dictator Saddam Hussein in 2005 resulted in a period of instability during which extremely valuable artifacts were looted from the museums in Baghdad. Many of those artifacts shed light on the world of the Bible. And some of them appear to be lost forever, despite the occasional good fortune in artifact recovery.

In the debate over the historical reliability of the Bible, archaeology appears to be tipping the scales to the right. Those who question the reliability of the Bible would do well to examine their own presuppositions. This is not to say that we should not continue to look critically at the text of the Bible and ancient artifacts. It is only by rigorous examination that we can present to the world evidence that demands a verdict.

Endnotes

Preface

[1] Dr. Craig Evans and scholars from Acadia University in Nova Scotia led this project.

Chapter 1: Geography and Chronology

[2] Many people believe that the Shechemites were related in some way to Abraham and his descendants. The patriarchs spent considerable time at Shechem and in the nearby region. Once the conquest began under Joshua, the Shechemites assimilated into the Israelite confederation. Bryant G. Wood, "The Role of Shechem in the Conquest of Canaan," in *To Understand the Scriptures: Essays in Honor of William H. Shea*, ed. David Merling (Berrien Springs, MI: Andrews University Press, 1997), 245–56.

[3] Amihai Mazar, *Archaeology of the Land of the Bible, 10,000–586 B.C.E.* (New York: Doubleday, 1990), 2–3. This book is one of the most significant and comprehensive contributions in the past generation to our understanding the archaeology of the Levant.

[4] The modern inhabitants—the Israelis on the west and the Jordanians on the east—irrigate heavily from the Jordan. Their drip irrigation system uses about 1 percent of the water per capita that American consumers use.

[5] Walter E. Rast, *Through the Ages in Palestinian Archaeology: An Introductory Handbook* (Philadelphia: Trinity Press International, 1992), 83–85.

[6] Currently there are negotiations underway to build a pipeline that would bring water from the Gulf of Aqaba to the Dead Sea in order to restore the water levels.

[7] The inscription was discovered in 1880 while the region was still under Ottoman rule. It resides in the Istanbul Archaeological Museum.

[8] Today, Caesarea Maritima is an underwater marvel that has been turned into the world's first underwater museum. Divers, not just scholars or marine archaeologists, take self-guided tours of the foundations of the harbor, the lighthouse, and a shipwreck. Underwater work at the site has been going on for over forty years by the University of Haifa.

[9] The year 2017 marked the final season of excavation at Gezer and Tel Lachish. Steve Ortiz led the Gezer dig on behalf of the Southwestern Baptist Theological Seminary. The Lachish dig was led by Michael Hasel on behalf of the Southern Adventist Seminary, along with Yosie Garfinkel of Hebrew University, and Martin Klingbeil.

[10] The pottery and artifacts from Timnahʿ are on display at the Tandy Archaeological Museum at Southwestern Baptist Theological Seminary in Fort Worth, Texas. George Kelm and Amihai Mazar excavated the site. Volunteers from the seminary also excavated Gezer.

[11] The first season of excavation began in December 2005. Collins plans to continue winter excavations at the site through the 2020 season.

[12] David E. Graves and Scott Stripling, "Re-examination of the Location for the Ancient City of Livias," *Levant* 43, no. 2 (Autumn 2011): 178–200.

[13] Petra may also be the site of Sela, which was captured by Amaziah (2 Kgs 14:7). It lies in the ancient territory of Edom and in the modern land of Jordan. The site gained worldwide popularity via the movie *Indiana Jones and the Last Crusade*, part of which was filmed there. The Nabateans were polytheistic, but their primary deity was Dushara. The impressive Temple of Treasures may have been the tomb of Aretas IV who is referred to in 2 Cor 11:32. Aretas' daughter married Herod Antipas. He divorced her so that he could marry Herodias, the wife of his brother Philip. John the Baptist was executed as a result of his objection to this wife swap.

[14] Later, John Lubbock (1834–1913) subdivided the Stone Age into the Paleolithic and Neolithic periods. The Paleolithic period preceded the Neolithic period in his scheme. John Lubbock, *Prehistoric Times as Illustrated by Ancient Remains: And the Manners and Customs of Modern Savages* (1865; repr., Cambridge: Cambridge University Press, 2010).

Chapter 2: Archaeological Fieldwork and Methodology

[15] Henry Hitchings, "Defining the World," *Biblical Archaeology Review* 32, no. 4 (August 2006): 10.

[16] John Wilkinson, trans., *Egeria's Travels*, 3rd ed. (Warminster: Aris & Phillips, 1999).

[17] William Lithgow, *The Totall Discourse of the Rare Aduentures…* (London, 1632).

[18] Ida Laura Pfeiffer, *Visit to the Holy Land, Egypt, and Italy*, trans. Henry William Dulcken, 4th ed. (London, 1862).

[19] W. F. Albright, *From the Stone Age to Christianity: Monotheism and the Historical Process* (Baltimore: Johns Hopkins University Press, 1940).

[20] W. F. Albright to David Livingston, February 23, 1970, in *Khirbet Nisya: The Search for Biblical Ai, 1979-2002; Excavation of the Site with Related Studies in Biblical Archaeology*, by David Livingston (Manheim, PA: Associates for Biblical Research, 2003), 263.

[21] The discussion of Ai is adapted from Scott Stripling and Mark Hassler, "The 'Problem' of Ai in Joshua 7–8: Solved after Nearly Forty Years of Excavation in the West Bank of Israel," *Bible and Spade* (in press).

[22] Genesis 4:17 refers to the city of Enoch, but to date no ruins have been found that could be associated with this city.

[23] Eilat Mazar, *The Palace of King David: Excavations at the Summit of the City of David; Preliminary Report of Seasons 2005–*

2007 (Jerusalem: Shoham Academic Research and Publication, 2009). Eilat Mazar is the granddaughter of the renowned Israeli archaeologist Benjamin Mazar.

[24] William G. Dever, *Who Were the Early Israelites and Where Did They Come From?* (Grand Rapids: Eerdmans, 2003), 45.

[25] Wood summarizes his position:

> I first became interested in Jericho while working on my Ph.D. dissertation on Canaanite pottery of the Late Bronze Age.... I would occasionally thumb through Garstang's preliminary reports to see if there was anything of interest. I became intrigued by a considerable amount of what appeared to be Late Bronze I (c. 1550–1400 B.C.E.) pottery he (Garstang) had excavated. This was precisely the period Kenyon repeatedly said was absent at Jericho! Because of the lack of precision in Garstang's fieldwork and the rambling nature of his preliminary reports, it was not possible to gain a clear picture of the stratigraphic sequence at Jericho from Garstang's work alone. Kenyon's conclusion, on the other hand, could not be checked because her work remained unpublished.
>
> After completing my dissertation in 1985, I decided to pursue the matter further, since by this time the Jericho reports were available.
>
> There is little doubt that Kenyon was correct in dating the double wall on top of the tell to the Early Bronze Age.
>
> In this she was right and Garstang wrong. But there is a serious question about her dating of the destruction of the residential area of the final Bronze Age city (Garstang's City IV) to the end of the Middle Bronze Age. Here I believe that Garstang was right after all!

Kenyon based her opinion almost exclusively on the absence of pottery imported from Cyprus and common to the Late Bronze I period.... Kenyon's analysis was based on what was not found at Jericho rather than what was found. It is methodologically unsound and indeed unacceptable.... She based her dating on the fact that she failed to find expensive, imported pottery in a small excavation area in an impoverished part of a city located far from major trade routes! Rather than unusual imported wares, attention should be given to the ordinary domestic pottery that Kenyon and Garstang both found in abundance. (Bryant Wood, "Did The Israelites Conquer Jericho? A New Look at the Archaeological Evidence," *Biblical Archaeology Review* 16, no. 2 [March–April 1990]: 50–51)

[26] William G. Dever, *What Did the Biblical Writers Know and When Did They Know It? What Archaeology Can Tell Us About the Reality of Ancient Israel* (Grand Rapids: Eerdmans, 2001), 26.

[27] Walter E. Rast, *Through the Ages in Palestinian Archaeology: An Introductory Handbook* (Philadelphia: Trinity Press International, 1992), 10.

[28] David Ussishkin, "A Synopsis of the Stratigraphical, Chronological and Historical Issues," in *The Renewed Archaeological Excavations at Lachish (1973-1994)*, ed. David Ussishkin, Tel Aviv University Sonia and Marco Nadler Institute of Archaeology Monograph Series 22 (Tel Aviv: Tel Aviv University Press, 2004), 1:90–92.

[29] Larry G. Herr and Gary L. Christopherson, *Excavation Manual: Madaba Plains Project*, rev. ed., ed. Philip R. Drey, with contributions by Randall W. Younker and David Merling (Berrien Springs: MI: Andrews University Press, 1998).

Chapter 3: Pre-patriarchal and Patriarchal Ages

[30] Victor H. Matthews and Don C. Benjamin, *Old Testament Parallels: Laws and Stories from the Ancient Near East*, 4th ed. (New York: Paulist, 2016).

[31] Narmer (Nemes) ruled Egypt around 3000 BC. He was the first to unite Upper Egypt and Lower Egypt as attested by the Narmer Palette that portrays him as wearing both crowns.

[32] Walter E. Rast, *Through the Ages in Palestinian Archaeology: An Introductory Handbook* (Philadelphia: Trinity Press International, 1992), 83–85.

[33] Older schemes referred to this period as Early Bronze IV and Middle Bronze I, but there are no discernable differences in the material remains.

[34] Tell Iktanu lies northeast of the Dead Sea, between Teleilat el-Ghassul and Tell el-Ḥammam.

[35] The book of Job, composed between 2100 BC and 1900 BC, also belongs to this period. For support of a patriarchal dating, see Bruce K. Waltke, *An Old Testament Theology: An Exegetical, Canonical, and Thematic Approach*, with Charles Yu (Grand Rapids: Zondervan, 2007), 927n1.

[36] The Masoretic Text (Textus Receptus) was written in Hebrew, whereas the Septuagint (250–50 BC) was written in Greek.

[37] Another potential drawback of identifying Sodom as Tell el-Ḥammam is Jeremiah 50:40, which indicates that Sodom remained barren after its destruction. Tell el-Ḥammam, however, only sat unoccupied for a short time during the Late Bronze Age.

Chapter 4: The Middle Bronze Age

[38] Shechem's Middle Bronze II wall was 9.4 feet (2.85 meters) wide at the base, and 8.7 feet (2.65 meters) wide at the top of the preserved height of 6.6 feet (2 meters). The Middle Bronze III wall

was 13 feet (4 meters) wide at the base and 6.6 feet (2 meters) wide at the top of the preserved height of 26 feet (8 meters).

[39] Douglas Petrovich, *The World's Oldest Alphabet: Hebrew as the Language of the Proto-Consonantal Script* (Jerusalem: Carta, 2016).

Chapter 5: The Late Bronze Age

[40] Douglas Petrovich, "Amenhotep II and the Historicity of the Exodus Pharaoh," *The Master's Seminary Journal* 17, no. 1 (Spring 2006): 81–110.

[41] William G. Dever, *Who Were the Early Israelites and Where Did They Come From?* (Grand Rapids: Eerdmans, 2003), 45–46.

[42] George L. Kelm, *Escape to Conflict* (Fort Worth, TX: IAR Publications, 1991). I interviewed Dr. Kelm in March 2005 at his home in San Antonio, Texas.

[43] Gary A. Byers, "New Evidence from Egypt on the Location of the Exodus Sea Crossing," pts. 1 and 2, *Bible and Spade* 19, no. 1 (Winter 2006): 14–22; no. 2 (Spring 2006): 34–40. Byers effectively argues the case for *yam sûp* as "the Sea of Reeds."

[44] The identification of Kadesh Barnea links to Thomas Edward Lawrence (Lawrence of Arabia, 1888–1935), who trained as an archaeologist at Jesus College, Oxford. He worked as a foreman for C. Leonard Woolley, who later discovered Ur of the Chaldees. Lawrence copied inscriptions, photographed finds, catalogued discoveries, bought antiquities, and used his mechanical ingenuity to solve small problems that would arise. As an apprentice at Carchemish, Lawrence increased his knowledge of archaeology and made worthy contributions of his own. He also took part in covering up a spying expedition—a precursor of things to come. When World War I broke out in August of 1914, Lawrence and Woolley were in England. They were told to finish their report on the survey of the Wilderness of Zin expedition quickly, to make the survey appear to have been solely archaeological in intent. While subscribers to the Palestine Exploration Fund publications

received Woolley and Lawrence's archaeological report, titled *The Wilderness of Zin*, Newcombe's detailed maps and photos of the area went to the British military. The surprising thing is that this rushed book, designed as a cover for a relatively brief spying survey, remains important in biblical studies. It identified the northern Sinai site of ʿAin el-Qudeirat, rather than nearby ʿAin Kadeis (a previous proposal), as the site of biblical Kadesh Barnea, where the Hebrews in the exodus settled and from whence Moses sent men to spy out the land of Canaan (Deut 1:2, 19; 2:1; Num 13:3–21). The front matter lists Lawrence as the chief author of the chapter on Kadesh Barnea (chapter 4). Even the respected Israeli archaeologist Rudolph Cohen agreed with the arguments of Lawrence and Woolley about the identification of the site.

[45] The excavations at Khirbet en-Nahas show Edomite statehood at the transition from the Late Bronze Age to Iron Age I. Levy based his dating on advanced radiocarbon methodology. In the 1930s, Nelson Glueck estimated the settlements in the area to be Iron Age I based on surface sherding at Khirbet en-Nahas and other (smaller) mining sites nearby. Either way, there were Edomites around for David to fight. The attempts to prove that Edom did not exist as a state until the seventh century (as an Assyrian vassal) reveal one's presuppositions. For some scholars, the Bible is guilty until proven innocent. Once again, these scholars have been proven wrong.

[46] Anson Rainey, "Shasu or Habiru: Who Were the Early Israelites?" *Biblical Archaeology Review* 34, no. 6 (November–December 2008): 51.

[47] Edward Robinson executed several probes at Jericho in 1867 and 1868. From these probes, he proved that the mound was artificial.

[48] Scott Stripling and Mark Hassler, "The 'Problem' of Ai in Joshua 7–8: Solved after Nearly Forty Years of Excavation in the West Bank of Israel," *Bible and Spade* (in press).

[49] Adam Zertal, "Ebal, Mount," in *The New Encyclopedia of Archaeological Excavations in the Holy Land*, ed. Ephraim Stern (New York: Simon & Schuster, 1993), 1:375–77.

[50] Brian Neil Peterson, "The Kh. el-Maqatir Ram's Head: Evidence of the Israelite Destruction of Ai?" *Near East Archaeological Society Bulletin* 61 (2016): 44–59.

[51] Scott Stripling, "The Israelite Tabernacle at Shiloh," *Bible and Spade* 29, no. 3 (Fall 2016): 88–95.

Chapter 6: The Iron Age

[52] Moses commanded the Israelites to build guardrails on their roofs to keep people from falling off (Deut 22:8). Psalm 129:6 refers to grass roofs in the Iron Age.

[53] Israel Finkelstein and Neil Asher Silberman, *The Bible Unearthed: Archaeology's New Vision of Ancient Israel and the Origin of Its Sacred Texts* (New York: Free Press, 2001), 112–13.

[54] When the same procedure is applied after the vessel is fired, it is referred to as wash.

[55] Israel Finkelstein, "Shiloh Yields Some, But Not All, of Its Secrets: Location of Tabernacle Still Uncertain," *Biblical Archaeology Review* 12, no. 1 (January–February 1986): 41.

[56] Shlomo Hellwing, Moshe Sade, and Vered Kishon, "Faunal Remains," in *Shiloh: The Archaeology of a Biblical Site*, by Israel Finkelstein, Shlomo Bunimovitz, and Zvi Lederman, with contributions by Baruch Brandl et al., ed. Israel Finkelstein, Sonia Marco Nadler Institute of Archaeology 10 (Tel Aviv: Tel Aviv University Press, 1993), 319.

[57] Prior to the united monarchy, there are obviously fewer direct synchronisms between the biblical text and the archaeological record. Most architecture and inscriptions result from some form of governmental centralization.

[58] A volunteer spotted this inscription in secondary usage as part of a later wall. The minimalists who had previously denied the existence of David were forced to admit that he existed and that he had a kingdom. They continue, however, to maintain that David's kingdom was an insignificant feudal-type estate in the central hill country.

[59] The foundations of the Samaritan temple are still standing. The few remaining Samaritans (about four hundred of them) continue to practice animal sacrifices there.

[60] David E. Graves, *Key Themes of the Old Testament: A Survey of Major Theological Themes* (Moncton, NB: Electronic Christian Media, 2013), 272–73.

[61] Kyle McCarter claimed that the king pictured is actually Joram. See P. Kyle McCarter, "Yaw, Son of 'Omri': A Philological Note on Israelite Chronology," *Bulletin of the American Schools of Oriental Research*, no. 216 (December 1974), 5–7. However, Galil opposes this interpretation on linguistic grounds. Gershon Galil, *The Chronology of the Kings of Israel and Judah*, Studies in the History and Culture of the Ancient Near East 9 (Leiden: Brill, 1996), 33n2.

[62] In the ancient Near East, the heir of a despot often entered into a coregency arrangement with his father. There would be two kings ruling, in effect. This practice complicates our understanding of the chronology of the biblical kings.

[63] The region of their origination is confirmed by both the Bible (Amos 9:7; Jer 47:4) and by the similarity in material culture of the Philistines and the residents of Mycenae and Crete.

Chapter 7: The Babylonian, Persian, and Hellenistic Ages

[64] Jeremiah 37:7–8 states, "Pharaoh's army, which has marched out to support you, will go back to its own land, to Egypt. Then the Babylonians will return and attack this city; they will capture it and burn it down."

Chapter 8: The Early Roman Age

[65] Frankie Snyder, Gabriel Barkay, and Zachi Dvira, "What the Temple Mount Floor Looked Like," *Biblical Archaeology Review* 42, no. 6 (November–December 2016): 56–59.

[66] David E. Graves and Scott Stripling, "Re-examination of the Location for the Ancient City of Livias," *Levant* 43, no. 2 (Autumn 2011): 178–200.

[67] Scott Stripling, "חירבת אל־מקטיר: בגבול בנימין–אפרים [Khirbet el-Maqatir: On the boarder of Benjamin–Ephraim]," *Qadmoniot* 48, no. 150 (December 2015): 78–83; Scott Stripling, "Have We Walked in the Footsteps of Jesus? Exciting New Possibilities at Khirbet el-Maqatir," *Bible and Spade* 27, no. 4 (Fall 2014): 88–94.

[68] Some recent scholars such as Colin J. Hamer have questioned this interpretation and proposed that more likely it refers to the role of Pergamon as the center of emperor worship. The strength of this interpretation resides in its recognition of the historical and textual context. Hamer also mentions the cult of Asclepius as a possible meaning behind the reference in Rev 2.

[69] David E. Graves, *Biblical Archaeology*, vol. 2, *Famous Discoveries That Support the Reliability of the Bible* (Toronto: Electronic Christian Media, 2015), 167–69; Donald T. Ariel, "Coins from the Synagogue at 'En Nashut," *Israel Exploration Journal* 37, no. 2–3 (1987): 147–57.

[70] Craig A. Evans, *Jesus and the Remains of His Day: Studies in Jesus and the Evidence of Material Culture* (Peabody, MA: Hendrickson, 2015), 253. Dr. Evans kindly mentions me in the preface to this magnificent work.

[71] Dan Levene, "'… and by the name of Jesus …': An Unpublished Magic Bowl in Jewish Aramaic," *Jewish Studies Quarterly* 6, no. 4 (1999): 283–308.

[72] Cestius Gallus began the siege but was relieved for incompetence and replaced by Vespasian. After Nero's suicide in AD 68 in the middle of the war and the quick demise of his three

successors (Otho, Galba, and Vitellius), Vespasian was recalled to Rome to be appointed Caesar, thus ending the Julio-Claudian dynasty and beginning the Flavian dynasty. Vespasian left his son Titus (who would become emperor upon his father's death) to complete the destruction of Jerusalem.

[73] Many of the antiquities that were excavated prior to the British Mandate in 1918 which effectively gave the British control over the land of the Bible after World War I ended up in the Istanbul Archaeological Museum because the Ottoman Empire ruled the entire Levant.

[74] Many archaeological sites in Jerusalem lie underneath the modern city. Excavated areas are protected from the level above by large steel beams, etc.

[75] The amazing ruins at Masada are showing signs of stress. A joint team from Beersheba's Ben-Gurion University of the Negev and the University of California-Berkeley monitors the areas of concern and takes corrective measures. The engineers involved with this project illustrate the interdisciplinary nature of the new archaeology.

Chapter 9: The Byzantine Age

[76] Alexander Schmemann, *The Historical Road of Eastern Orthodoxy*, trans. Lynda W. Kesich (1963; repr., Crestwood, NY: St. Vladimir's Seminary Press, 1997), 62.

[77] Ibid.

[78] Vassilios Tzaferis, "Inscribed 'To God Jesus Christ': Early Christian Prayer Hall Found in Megiddo Prison," *Biblical Archaeology Review* 33, no. 2 (March–April 2007): 38–49.

[79] Mark Rose, "Early Church at Aqaba," *Archaeology* 51, no. 6 (November–December 1998): 18.

[80] Discussion adapted from Gary A. Byers and Scott Stripling, "Those Indefatigable Byzantines!" *Bible and Spade* 26, no. 4 (Fall 2013): 108–112.

Conclusion

[81] Walter E. Rast, *Through the Ages in Palestinian Archaeology: An Introductory Handbook* (Philadelphia: Trinity Press International, 1992), 1.

Glossary

anachronism. A person or thing that is chronologically out of place.

anthropoid. Shaped like or resembling a man.

ashlar. A large-shaped stone set against another. Often used in large foundations.

balk. In an archaeological square, a strip of unexcavated earth. The vertical face shows the stratigraphy.

bulla. (plural: bullae) A lump of clay with an impression on it used to seal ancient correspondence.

carination. A pronounced or sharp curve on pottery or glassware.

contamination. The accidental blending of one locus with another.

dendrochronology. The science of measuring dates by the study of growth rings in trees and shrubs.

epigraphy. The study of ancient inscriptions.

epitaph. Words inscribed on a tomb or burial vault in memory of the deceased.

glacis. (plural: glacis) A defensive slope that ascends to a city's fortification.

glyptic art. A carving on small stones or gems, often on seals or amulets.

hegemony. Political and military dominance and control.

in situ. ("in place") In the original location. An undisturbed context.

khirbet. (Arabic) A designation for an ancient site in which some ruins are visible (e.g., Khirbet Qumran) but not a built-up mound (cp. Tell).

kiln. An industrial oven used for drying, baking, or hardening.

levigation. A process of removing small stones and other impurities from clay prior to casting a pottery vessel.

locus. (plural: loci) A distinguishable archaeological feature at an archaeological site, such as an earth layer, wall, subterranean structure.

maṣēbâ. (plural: *maṣēbôt*) A standing stone, usually for cultic purposes.

megalith. A large stone

mikvah. (plural: mikvaot) A baptistery used for ritual purification.

minimalist. A scholar who presupposes that much of the material in the Old Testament is non-historical.

necropolis. A cemetery or burial place.

numismatics. The study of coins.

obelisk. An inscribed stone monument often describing a king's victory.

orthostat. A large slab that is often carved and used to decorate palaces or temples.

ossuary. A box used for storing the bones of a corpse after the flesh has decayed.

ostracon. (plural: ostraca) Writing on a broken piece of pottery.

pithos. (plural: pithoi) A large ceramic storage jar.

sherd. (British spelling: shard) A broken piece of pottery.

stele. (plural: stelae) A stone symbolizing the sun god Ra, inscribed with religious and commemorative statements.

stratigraphy. The layering of strata at an archaeological site.

synchronism. An agreement between the archaeological data and the biblical text.

tectonic plate. The expansive sections of earth layer that comprise the earth's outer shell.

tell. (Arabic: tell; Hebrew: tel) A stratified mound that grows through the centuries as people build and rebuild cities.

temenos. The sacred area of a temple.

terra-cotta. Reddish ceramic (earthenware) material.

topography. The layout of natural or man-made surface features of a region.

typology. In archaeology, the study of various forms, whether pottery, glass, flint, or other materials.

vassal. A person or country subservient to a suzerain.

wadi. (Arabic: wadi; Hebrew: naḥal) A dry riverbed that can facilitate flash floods.

Bibliography

Aharoni, Yohanan. *The Land of the Bible: A Historical Geography.* Rev. ed. Translated and edited by A. F. Rainey. Philadelphia: Westminster, 1979.

Albright, W. F. *From the Stone Age to Christianity: Monotheism and the Historical Process.* Baltimore: Johns Hopkins University Press, 1940.

Aling, Charles F. *Egypt and Bible History: From Earliest Times to 1000 B.C.* Baker Studies in Biblical Archaeology. Grand Rapids: Baker Books, 1981.

Archaeological Study Bible: An Illustrated Walk through Biblical History and Culture. Grand Rapids: Zondervan, 2006.

Avi-Yonah, Michael, ed. *Encyclopedia of Archaeological Excavations in the Holy Land.* 4 vols. Englewood Cliffs, NJ: Prentice Hall, 1975.

Ben-Tor, Amnon, ed. *The Archaeology of Ancient Israel.* Translated by R. Greenberg. New Haven: Yale University Press, 1992.

Dever, William G. *What Did the Biblical Writers Know and When Did They Know It? What Archaeology Can Tell Us About the Reality of Ancient Israel.* Grand Rapids: Eerdmans, 2001.

―――. *Who Were the Early Israelites and Where Did They Come From?* Grand Rapids: Eerdmans, 2003.

Dothan, Trude. *The Philistines and Their Material Culture.* New Haven: Yale University Press, 1982.

Evans, Craig A. *From Jesus to the Church: The First Christian Generation.* Louisville: Westminster John Knox, 2014.

―――. *Jesus and His World: The Archaeological Evidence.* Louisville: Westminster John Knox, 2012.

―――. *Jesus and the Remains of His Day: Studies in Jesus and the Evidence of Material Culture.* Peabody, MA: Hendrickson, 2015.

Ferguson, Everett. *Backgrounds of Early Christianity.* 3rd ed. Grand Rapids: Eerdmans, 2003.

Finegan, Jack. *Archaeological History of the Ancient Middle East.* Boulder, CO: Westview, 1979.

Finkelstein, Israel, and Neil Asher Silberman. *The Bible Unearthed: Archaeology's New Vision of Ancient Israel and the Origin of Its Sacred Texts.* New York: Free Press, 2001.

Freedman, David Noel, and David Frank Graf, eds. *Palestine in Transition: The Emergence of Ancient Israel*. Sheffield: Almond Press, 1983.

Gibson, Shimon. *The Final Days of Jesus: The Archaeological Evidence*. New York: HarperCollins, 2009.

Glueck, Nelson. *The Other Side of the Jordan*. 2nd ed. Cambridge: American Schools of Oriental Research, 1970.

Grant, Michael. *The History of Ancient Israel*. New York: Scribner's Sons, 1984.

Graves, David E. *Biblical Archaeology*. Vol. 1, *An Introduction with Recent Discoveries That Support the Reliability of the Bible*. Toronto: Electronic Christian Media, 2014.

Halpern, Baruch. *The Emergence of Israel in Canaan*. Society of Biblical Literature Monograph Series 29. Chico, CA: Scholars Press, 1983.

Harding, Lankester G. *The Antiquities of Jordan*. Rev. ed. London: Lutterworth, 1967.

Hemer, Colin J. *The Letters to the Seven Churches of Asia in their Local Setting*. Biblical Resource Series. Grand Rapids: Eerdmans, 1989.

Hendin, David. *Guide to Biblical Coins*. With values by Herbert Kreindler. 5th ed. New York: Amphora Books, 2010.

Hoerth, Alfred J. *Archaeology and the Old Testament*. Grand Rapids: Baker Books, 1998.

Hoffmeier, James K. *Israel in Egypt: The Evidence for the Authenticity of the Exodus Tradition*. New York: Oxford University Press, 1995.

House, Wayne H. *Chronological and Background Charts of the New Testament*. 2nd ed. Grand Rapids: Zondervan, 2009.

Kaiser, Walter C., Jr., and Paul D. Wegner. *A History of Israel: From the Bronze Age through the Jewish Wars*. 2nd ed. Nashville: Broadman & Holman, 2017.

Kelm, George L. *Escape to Conflict*. Fort Worth, TX: IAR Publications, 1991.

Kempinski, Aharon, and Ronny Reich, eds. *The Architecture of Ancient Israel: From the Prehistoric to the Persian Periods; In Memory of Immanuel (Munya) Dunayevsky*. Jerusalem: Israel Exploration Society, 1992.

Khouri, Rami G. *The Antiquities of the Jordan Rift Valley*. Amman: Al Kutba, 1988.

King, Philip J., and Lawrence E. Stager. *Life in Biblical Israel*. Louisville: Westminster John Knox, 2001.

Kitchen, Kenneth A. *The Bible in Its World: The Bible and Archaeology Today.* Downers Grove, IL: InterVarsity Press, 1978.

———. *On the Reliability of the Old Testament.* Grand Rapids: Eerdmans, 2001.

Magness, Jodi. *Stone and Dung, Oil and Spit: Jewish Daily Life in the Time of Jesus.* Grand Rapids: Eerdmans, 2011.

Matthews, Victor H., and Don C. Benjamin. *Old Testament Parallels: Laws and Stories from the Ancient Near East.* 4th ed. New York: Paulist, 2016.

Mazar, Amihai. *Archaeology of the Land of the Bible, 10,000–586 B.C.E.* New York: Doubleday, 1990.

McCarter, P. Kyle, Jr. "The Patriarchal Age: Abraham, Isaac, and Jacob," revised by Ronald S. Hendel. In *Ancient Israel: From Abraham to the Roman Destruction of the Temple.* 3rd ed. Edited by Hershel Shanks, 1–34. Washington, DC: Biblical Archaeology Society, 2010.

McCray, John R. *Archaeology and the New Testament.* Grand Rapids: Baker Books, 1991.

Meyers, Eric M., ed. *The Oxford Encyclopedia of Archaeology in the Near East.* 5 vols. New York: Oxford University Press, 1997.

Miller, J. Maxwell, and John H. Hayes. *A History of Ancient Israel and Judah.* Louisville: Westminster John Knox, 2006.

Petrovich, Douglas. *The World's Oldest Alphabet: Hebrew as the Language of the Proto-Consonantal Script.* Jerusalem: Carta, 2016.

Price, Randall. *The Stones Cry Out: What Archaeology Reveals About the Truth of the Bible.* Eugene, OR: Harvest House, 1997.

Rasmussen, Carl G. *Zondervan Atlas of the Bible.* Rev. ed. Grand Rapids: Zondervan, 2010.

Rast, Walter E. *Through the Ages in Palestinian Archaeology: An Introductory Handbook.* Philadelphia: Trinity Press International, 1992.

Ritmeyer, Leen. *The Quest: Revealing the Temple Mount in Jerusalem.* Jerusalem: Carta, 2006.

Romer, John. *The History of Archaeology: Great Excavations of the World.* New York: Checkmark, 2001.

Schlegel, William. *Satellite Bible Atlas: Historical Geography of the Bible.* N.p., 2012.

Sharon, Moshe. *The Holy Land in History and Thought: Papers Submitted to the International Conference on the Relations between the Holy Land and the World Outside It.* Leiden: Brill, 1997.

Soden, Wolfram von. *The Ancient Orient: An Introduction to the Study of the Ancient Near East.* Grand Rapids: Eerdmans, 1994.

Soggin, Alberto J. *A History of Ancient Israel: From the Beginnings to the Bar Kochba Revolt, A.D. 135.* Philadelphia: Westminster, 1984.

Stern, Ephraim, ed. *The New Encyclopedia of Archaeological Excavations in the Holy Land.* 5 vols. Jerusalem, 1993, 2008.

Thiele, Edwin R. *The Mysterious Numbers of the Hebrew Kings.* Rev. ed. Grand Rapids: Kregel, 1983.

Thompson, Henry O. *Biblical Archaeology: The World, Mediterranean, the Bible.* New York: Paragon, 1987.

Walton, John H. *Chronological and Background Charts of the Old Testament.* Rev. ed. Grand Rapids: Zondervan, 1994.

Illustration Credits

The following photographic credits indicate ownership of the original prints used with permission to publish the black and white photographs. Numbers refer to the photograph number in the text. Appreciation to the sources named for permission to publish the following photographs.

Altes Museum, Berlin (Pedersen, Gunnar Bach, PD): fig. 7.5 (*background removed*)
Bible and Spade archive: fig. 5.5
Bible Odyssey at www.bibleodyssey.org: fig. 6.10
© Bolen, Todd (photograph courtesy of www.BiblePlaces.com): fig. 6.1
© Copyright the Trustees of the British Museum, London, England
    Photographs by David Graves: figs. 3.1, 6.9, 7.2, 7.3
    Photograph by Willis: fig. 6.8
Creative Commons. CC-BY-SA 3.0. Public Domain (PD)
    Aleks, Nenya: fig. 7.1
    Ceedjee: fig. 2.6
    Hanay: fig. 5.1
    Hillewaert, Hans: fig. 2.2
    Moody, Jacob: fig. 4.1
    Kramer, Barry: fig. 5.6 (photo overlay Steven Rudd)
    Pedersen, Gunnar Bach: fig. 7.5 (background removed)
    Willis: fig. 6.8
    www.civilization.org.uk PD-Art.: fig. 2.4
Daughtry, Terry: fig. 2.3 (*right*)
Davis, John: fig. 8.3
© Graves, David (photographs courtesy of): figs. 1.6, 1.8, 1.9, 2.1, 2.3 (*left*), 2.5, 3.1, 4.2, 4.5, 5.2, 5.3, 5.4, 6.6, 6.9, 6.11 (*left*), 6.12 (*drawing*), 7.2, 7.3, 8.2, 8.4, 8.6, 8.7, 8.8, 8.9, 9.3
Kelm, George: fig. 1.5
Leavitt, Abigail: fig. 3.3
© Luddeni, Michael (photographs courtesy of): figs. 1.3, 2.9, 3.2, 4.4, 6.11 (*right*), 7.4, 8.1, 8.5, 8.11, 8.12, 9.1
Nimi, Ani: fig. 4.3
Oriental Institute of the University of Chicago: fig. 3.4
© Ritmeyer, Leen (drawings courtesy of): figs. 2.8, 6.2, 6.3, 9.2
Royal Ontario Museum (photograph by David Graves): fig. 8.4
© Rudd, Steven (drawings courtesy of): table 3.1 (*data*); figs. 1.1, 1.2, 1.4, 1.7, 5.6 (*overlay only*)
Schlegel, Bill: fig. 6.7
Stripling, Scott: figs. 2.7, 6.4, 6.5, 8.10
University of Haifa, Department of Archaeology: fig. 5.1

Wright, Daniel: fig. 5.5 (*drawing*)

Index of Subjects

Index of Scripture
and Other Ancient Documents

Deuterocanonical Documents

Dead Sea Scrolls

Classical and Ancient Christian Documents

About the Author

Dr. Scott Stripling is provost and professor of biblical archaeology and church history at The Bible Seminary in Katy (Houston), Texas. He directs the ABR excavations at ancient Shiloh. A popular speaker and author, Dr. Stripling serves on the board of directors for the Near East Archaeological Society. He and his wife, Janet, have four children and two grandchildren.

CPSIA information can be obtained
at www.ICGtesting.com
Printed in the USA
BVHW042021220119
538392BV00003B/4/P